GALAXY OF COMING EVENTS, MEANING AND OUTCOME OF THIS EUROPEAN WAR, TERMINATING IN A WORLD CONFEDERATION, ACCORDING TO PROPHECY, THE BOOK OF REVELATION AS I SEE IT

Published @ 2017 Trieste Publishing Pty Ltd

ISBN 9780649590674

Galaxy of Coming Events, Meaning and Outcome of This European War, Terminating in a World Confederation, According to Prophecy, the Book of Revelation as I See It by William Francis Manley

Except for use in any review, the reproduction or utilisation of this work in whole or in part in any form by any electronic, mechanical or other means, now known or hereafter invented, including xerography, photocopying and recording, or in any information storage or retrieval system, is forbidden without the permission of the publisher, Trieste Publishing Pty Ltd, PO Box 1576 Collingwood, Victoria 3066 Australia.

All rights reserved.

Edited by Trieste Publishing Pty Ltd.
Cover @ 2017

This book is sold subject to the condition that it shall not, by way of trade or otherwise, be lent, re-sold, hired out, or otherwise circulated without the publisher's prior consent in any form or binding or cover other than that in which it is published and without a similar condition including this condition being imposed on the subsequent purchaser.

www.triestepublishing.com

WILLIAM FRANCIS MANLEY

GALAXY OF COMING EVENTS, MEANING AND OUTCOME OF THIS EUROPEAN WAR, TERMINATING IN A WORLD CONFEDERATION, ACCORDING TO PROPHECY, THE BOOK OF REVELATION AS I SEE IT

WILLIAM FRANCIS MANLEY

GALAXY OF COMING EVENTS,
MEANING AND OUTCOME OF THIS
EUROPEAN WAR, USA V. VATICAN
+ WORLD CONFEDERATION,
ACCORDING TO PROPHECY, THE BOOK
OF REVELATION, AS 1917

Trieste

GALAXY OF COMING EVENTS

MEANING AND OUTCOME
OF THIS

EUROPEAN WAR

TERMINATING IN A

WORLD CONFEDERATION

ACCORDING TO PROPHECY

THE BOOK OF REVELATION AS I SEE IT

BY

REV. WILLIAM FRANCIS MANLEY

A SERVANT OF THE

LORD JESUS CHRIST

W. F. MANLEY, *Publisher*
1616 New Jersey St.
Los Angeles, California
U. S. A.

Gift of author

Copyright 1918
William Francis Manley
Los Angeles, California
U. S. A.

CONTENTS

PREFACE	7
MEANING AND OUTCOME OF THIS EUROPEAN WAR	11
MR. TAFT WANTS NEW ALLIANCE POLICY	27
THREE YEARS OF WAR	31
THE REVELATION OF JESUS CHRIST	33
JOHN, TO THE SEVEN CHURCHES	36
THE KINGDOM OF HEAVEN	46
KEY TO THE BOOK OF REVELATION	52
THE BOOK OF REVELATION	54
THE SIGNS OF HIS COMING	59
JOHN CAUGHT UP INTO HEAVEN	71
A BOOK WITH SEVEN SEALS	81
OPENING THE SEVEN SEALS	89
THIS EUROPEAN WAR	98
THE ANTI-CHRIST	101
OPENING THE FIFTH SEAL	105
OPENING THE SIXTH SEAL	109
SEALING THE 144,000	114
OPENING THE SEVENTH SEAL	119
THE SEVEN TRUMPETS	121
OPENED THE BOTTOMLESS PIT	124

THE LAST WAR	128
THE SEVEN THUNDERS	132
THE TWO WITNESSES	135
CHRIST TAKES THE KINGDOM	142
THE WOMAN CLOTHED WITH THE SUN	145
THE MAN CHILD	150
THE SEVEN-HEADED BEAST	158
THE ECCLESIASTICAL BEAST	164
ANGELS PREACHING	168
THE FALSE PROPHET	172
THE DESTRUCTION OF THE WICKED	177
SEVEN LAST PLAGUES	179
THE SCARLET-COLORED BEAST	189
THE MARRIAGE OF THE LAMB	209
BINDING SATAN	216
THE GREAT WHITE THRONE	223
THE NEW EARTH	229
THE HOLY CITY	240
THE LITTLE HORN	247
THE STAR OF BETHLEHEM	256
THE EARTH LYING IN RUINS	259
ISRAEL TO BECOME A NATION	253

PREFACE

We have written this book under a deep sense of the seriousness, the awful consequences of changing anything in the Book of Revelation, and have waited on God continually for guidance in every word written that we may change nothing; but only to cause the reader to see what God has said therein, in connection with other scriptures on the same subject, thus showing an agreement, and not a difference.

We believe God has directed both mind and pen as we have been writing, and we have written this book, hoping to correct many incorrect things that have been said and written concerning the Book of Revelation.

For more than forty years, while preaching the gospel, we have read and rejected much that has been written on the Book of Revelation, because it did not agree with the Book itself.

For ten or more years we have at times contemplated writing thereon, but feared to do so. Four years ago we wrote on the first five chapters and was checked from proceeding farther. In August of 1917 it became very clear that we should finish the book, and send it out, as the time had come to give it to the world. We have continually, day and night, prayed to God that He would so control body, soul and spirit that not one statement should be made that was not correct and pleasing to Him. And now that it is written, we are saying to God, "If any statement we have written is displeasing to Thee, make it known, and the manuscript shall go into the fire."

If I have changed a word in this Book of Revelation, I did not mean to do so, and now ask God to forgive me.

THE AUTHOR.

Notice to All the Rulers of the Earth

On the 30th day of September, 1914, sixty days after the present war was declared, we mailed a printed copy of the following Notice of coming events, and the real meaning of this European war, to each and every one of the European Rulers; and to the President of the United States; and also sent copies to the Secretary of State, and Secretary of War, of the United States, together with a type-written note to each and all of them, calling their careful attention to the article. In October, 1914, we received the following notes:

Buckingham Palace, England.

The Private Secretary is commanded by the King to acknowledge the receipt of Mr. William Manley's letter of the 30th ult.

19th October, 1914.

(SEAL)   DEPARTMENT OF STATE,
                    WASHINGTON

Mr. William Francis Manley,
    111½ Winston Street,
        Los Angeles, California.

DEAR MR. MANLEY:

For Mr. Bryan I beg to acknowledge the receipt of your letter of September 30, with which you were so good as to send him a copy of an article with reference to the European war.

Very truly yours,
MANTON M. WYVELL,
Private Secretary.

During the first week in October, 1914, we mailed a copy of this same Article to every other Ruler we knew of on Earth.

The Meaning and Outcome of this European War

It is not the "last war." Neither does it presage the "end of the world."

Human beings will live upon this earth for a thousand years after the first resurrection has taken place. Rev. 20:1-5, R. V.

And I saw an angel coming down out of heaven, having the key of the abyss and a great chain in his hand. And he laid hold on the dragon, the old serpent, which is the Devil and Satan, and bound him for a thousand years, and cast him into the abyss, and shut it, and sealed it over him, that he should deceive the nations no more, until the thousand years should be finished: after this he must be loosed for a little time.

And I saw thrones, and they sat upon them, and judgment was given unto them: and I saw the souls of them that had been beheaded for the testimony of Jesus, and for the word of God, and such as worshipped not the beast, neither his image, and received not the mark upon their forehead and upon their hand; and they lived, and reigned with Christ a thousand years. The rest of the dead lived not until the thousand years should be finished. This is the first resurrection.

The first resurrection has not taken place yet. So we are at least one thousand years this side of the end of the world.

A war in which two hundred millions of men will go forth from Asia (beyond the Euphrates) to kill the third part of men, will follow this present European war. Rev. 9:14-18, R. V.

> One saying to the sixth angel that had the trumpet. Loose the four angels that are bound at the great river Euphrates. And the four angels were loosed, that had been prepared for the hour and day and month and year, that they should kill the third part of men. And the number of the armies of the horsemen was twice ten thousand times ten thousand: I heard the number of them. And thus I saw the horses in the vision, and them that sat on them, having breastplates as of fire and of hyacinth and of brimstone: and the heads of the horses are as the heads of lions; and out of their mouths proceedeth fire and smoke and brimstone. By these three plagues was the third part of men

killed, by the fire and the smoke and the brimstone, which proceeded out of their mouths.

This will probably come soon after its close, or it may be but a continuation of this war.

Then the great Armageddon Battle of God Almighty, closing up and putting an end to all human strife on the battlefield. When the Lord shall go forth on a white horse, followed by the armies in heaven upon white horses, to smite the nations and rule them with a rod of iron. Rev. 19:11-21, R. V.

And I saw the heaven opened; and behold, a white horse, and he that sat thereon called Faithful and True; and in righteousness he doth judge and make war. And his eyes are a flame of fire, and upon his head are many diadems; and he hath a name written which no one knoweth but he himself. And he is arrayed in a garment sprinkled with blood: and his name is called The Word of God. And the armies which are in heaven followed him upon white horses, clothed in fine linen, white and pure. And out of his mouth proceedeth a sharp sword, that with it he should smite the nations: and he shall rule them with a rod of iron: and he treadeth the winepress of the fierceness of the wrath of God, the Almighty. And he hath on his garment and on his thigh a name written, King of Kings, and Lord of Lords.

And I saw an angel standing in the sun; and he cried with a loud voice, saying to all the birds that fly in mid-heaven, Come and be gathered together unto the great supper of God; that ye may eat the flesh of kings, and the flesh of captains, and the flesh of mighty men, and the flesh of horses and of them that sit thereon, and the flesh of all men, both free and bond, and small and great.

And I saw the beast, and the Kings of the earth, and their armies gathered together to make war against him that sat upon the horse, and against his army. And the beast was taken, and with him the false prophet that wrought the signs in his sight, wherewith he deceived them that had received the mark of the beast and them that worshipped his image: they two were cast alive into the lake of fire that burneth with brimstone: and the rest were killed with the sword of him that sat upon the horse, even the sword which came forth out of his mouth; and all the birds were filled with their flesh.

Then all weapons of war will be made into plows and pruning hooks, and farm implements;

and men will learn war no more. For the Lord Jesus Christ will reign supreme on earth for a thousand years. Rev. 20:4-6.

The present European war, the greatest known in all history, is the beginning of the end of all human governments; and is clearly foretold in the Scriptures.

The Antichrist

It is the Anti-Christ war, in which he, the Anti-Christ, has gone forth to conquer the whole world.

> Now we beseech you, brethren, touching the coming of our Lord Jesus Christ, and our gathering together unto Him: to the end that ye be not quickly shaken from your mind, nor yet be troubled, either by spirit, or by word, or by epistle as from us, as that the day of the Lord is now present; let no man beguile you in any wise: for it will not be, except the falling away come first, and the man of sin be revealed, the son of perdition, he that opposeth and exalteth himself against all that is called God or that is worshipped; so that he sitteth in the temple of God, setting himself forth as God. Remember ye not, that, when I was yet with you, I told you these things? And now ye know that which restraineth, to the end that he may be revealed in his own

season. For the mystery of lawlessness doth already work: only there is one that restraineth now, until he be taken out of the way. And then shall be revealed the lawless one, whom the Lord Jesus shall slay with the breath of His mouth, and bring to naught by the manifestation of His coming; even he, whose coming is according to the working of Satan with all power and signs and lying wonders, and with all deceit of unrighteousness for them that perish; because they received not the love of the truth, that they might be saved. 2 Thess. 2:1-10, R. V.

The time has come for this man of sin or Anti-Christ to be revealed; and to set up his kingdom. The Anti-Christ could not come forth while God restrained, or held him back; and Christ will not return to the earth until the Anti-Christ be revealed and does his work, under the direct power of the Devil.

The restraining power of God has been removed, and he, the Anti-Christ, has gone forth on his white horse (Rev. 6:1-2) with the red war horse immediately following him. Rev. 6:1-4, R. V.

And I saw when the Lamb opened one of the seven seals, and I heard one of the four living creatures saying as with a voice of thunder, Come. And I saw, and behold, a white horse, and he that sat thereon had a bow; and there was given unto him a crown; and he came forth conquering, and to conquer.

And when he opened the second seal, I heard the second living creature saying, Come. And another horse came forth, a red horse; and to him that sat thereon it was given to take peace from the earth, and that they should slay one another: and there was given unto him a great sword.

Here is the beginning of the Anti-Christ war; and during this war one man will appear as the great central leader; and he will not be one of the King's Emperors, or Czar, but another King receiving his crown and throne from Satan. Rev. 13:2. "And the dragon gave him his power, and throne, and great authority." He will be the great leader at the close of the war, but not yet crowned.

And before him three of the nations entering this war will be annihilated, plucked up by the roots. Dan. 7:8. "I considered the horns, and behold, there came up among them another little horn, before whom there were three of the first horns plucked up by the roots * * * and of the ten horns that were in his head, and of the other which came up, and before whom three fell; even of that horn that had eyes, and a mouth that spake very great things, whose look was more stout than his fellows. * * * The ten horns out of this kingdom are ten kings [or kingdoms] that shall arise after them; and he shall be diverse from the first, and he shall subdue three kings [or kingdoms] and he shall speak great words against the Most High, and shall wear out the saints of the Most High, and think to change times and laws; and they shall be given into his hand until a time and times, and the dividing of time." This is the Anti-Christ.

At the closing of the war, the Anti-Christ will form a confederacy of ten kingdoms, with ten crowned heads.

And this confederacy of all Europe, and perhaps America, will conquer, and rule the whole world for three years and a half.

It will also set up a State religion, and put to death all persons who will not worship its god.

> And I saw a beast coming up out of the sea, having ten horns and seven heads, and on his horns ten diadems, and upon his heads names of blasphemy. And the beast which I saw was like unto a leopard, and his feet were as the feet of a bear, and his mouth as the mouth of a lion: and the dragon gave him his power, and his throne, and great authority. And I saw one of his heads as though it had been smitten unto death, and his deathstroke was

healed; and the whole earth wondered after the beast; and they worshipped the dragon, because he gave his authority unto the beast; and they worshipped the beast, saying, Who is like unto the beast? and who is able to war with him? And there was given to him a mouth speaking great things and blasphemies; and there was given to him authority to continue forty and two months. And he opened his mouth for blasphemies against God, to blaspheme His name, and His tabernacle, even them that dwell in the heaven. And it was given unto him to make war with the saints, and to overcome them: and there was given to him authority over every tribe and people and tongue and nation. And all that dwell on the earth shall worship him, every one whose name hath not been written in the Book of Life of the Lamb that hath been slain from the foundation of the world. If any man hath an ear, let him hear. If any man is for captivity, into captivity he goeth: if any man shall kill with the sword, with the sword must he be killed. Here is the patience and the faith of the saints. Rev. 13:1-10, R. V.

This Anti-Christ kingdom or confederacy will only continue for three years and six months, when the Lord Jesus will destroy it. Rev. 19:19-21. "And I saw the beast [the Anti-Christ] and the Kings of the Earth and their armies, gather together to make war against Him that sat on the horse, and against His army. And the beast was taken, and with him the false prophet that wrought miracles before him, with which he deceived them that had received the mark of the beast, and them that worshipped his image. These both were cast alive into a lake of fire burning with brimstone. And the remnant were slain with the sword of Him that sat upon the horse, which proceedeth out of His mouth, and all the fowls were filled with their flesh."

This is the ending of the Anti-Christ kingdom, or World Confederacy, over which the Man of Sin is to rule the whole Earth. And then, the Lord Jesus Christ, having destroyed the Anti-Christ and his followers, will raise up a people who will serve God for a thousand years.

Four Beasts

The Prophet Daniel saw in vision four great beasts coming up from the sea. The fourth beast was dreadful and terrible, and strong exceedingly; and it had great iron teeth; it devoured and break in pieces, and stamped the residue with its feet; and it was diverse from all the beasts that were before it; and it had ten horns. And behold! there came up among them another little horn before whom there were three of the first horns plucked up by the roots; and behold! in this horn were eyes like the eyes of a man, and a mouth speaking great things.

"I, Daniel, was grieved in my spirit in the midst of my body, and the vision of my head troubled me. I came near unto one of them that stood by, and asked him the truth of all this. So he told me, and made me know the interpretation of the things." Dan. 7:15-16. These four beasts represented the Babylonian, the Medo Persian, the Greek and the Roman Empires.

Then Daniel desired to know the truth of the fourth beast, and especially of the ten horns of this fourth beast; and of the other little horn, before whom three of the ten horns fell, or were plucked up by the roots. And Daniel was informed that "The fourth beast shall be the fourth kingdom upon the earth, which shall be diverse from all kingdoms, and shall tread it down, and break it in pieces. And the ten horns out of this kingdom are ten kings that shall arise; and another king shall arise after them; and he shall be diverse from the first, and he shall subdue three kings. And he shall speak great words against the Most High, and shall wear out the saints of the Most High, and think to change times and laws; and they shall be given into his hand until a time, and times and the dividing of times [three and a half years]. Dan. 7:23-25.

The ten horns of this fourth Roman Beast, monarchy, are the ten kingdoms that succeeded the Roman Empire, or the present European and Asiatic powers who hold the country formerly known as the Roman Empire.

The Little Horn, with man's eyes and man's mouth, was not any one of the ten original horns, but another horn, which came up after them, and among them. This is the Anti-Christ Kingdom which will come up and rule the whole earth for a short time. And this Anti-Christ rule will be the most cruel, blasphemous, diabolical rule ever known on earth.

If this war is the Anti-Christ war, as the writer firmly believes it is, there will be no peace until the Anti-Christ, and the war, famine and pestilence, and wild beasts of the earth, have desolated one-fourth part of the earth, which means three times the area of Europe.

> And when he opened the third seal, I heard the third living creature saying, Come. And I saw, and behold a black horse; and he that sat thereon had a balance in his hand. And I heard as it were a voice in the midst of the four living creatures saying. A measure of wheat for a penny, and three measures of barley

for a penny; and the oil and the wine hurt thou not.

And when he opened the fourth seal, I heard the voice of the fourth living creature saying, Come. And I saw and behold, a pale horse; and he that sat upon him, his name was Death; and Hades followed with him. And there was given unto them authority over the fourth part of the earth to kill with sword and famine, and with death, and by the wild beasts of the earth. Rev. 6:5-8, R. V.

This war will spread over all Europe, and part of Asia; and probably America; over one-fourth part of the Earth.

And famine, with all its horrors, will destroy millions of people.

Then pestilence will follow, taking millions more.

And until three of the contending nations are destroyed.

Then the Anti-Christ will form a confederacy of ten kingdoms, so shattered and weak that they will have no hope of ever regaining their places as independent kingdoms.

The Apostle Paul in referring to this Anti-Christ war said: "For when they shall say Peace and safety; then sudden destruction cometh upon them, as travail upon a woman with child, and they shall not escape." I Thess. 5:3.

All the outcry for peace will be of no avail. Men who will not serve God, are now turned over to the Devil, whom they have served. And awful destruction, at the hands of the Devil and his servant, the Anti-Christ, awaits them.

If this is the Anti-Christ war, three nations will fall to rise no more; and famine and pestilence will soon break out wherever the war spreads. And the wild beasts will break forth and devour helpless women and children.

We are rapidly going down into the great tribulation. If this is the Anti-Christ war of Rev. 6:1-8, the Anti-Christ will first be so revealed that true Christians will know him as the Anti-Christ. He must be revealed before our Lord's return to gather His saints unto Himself. II Thess. 2:3-4.

An Earthquake

Then a great earthquake will come, that will move every mountain and island out of their places, and the sun will become black as sackcloth of hair, and the moon will become as blood, and the stars of heaven will fall to the earth. Rev. 6:12-13.

These are given as signs of the immediate coming of the Lord Jesus. Matt. 24:29-51 and Mark 13:24-37, and Luke 21:25-36.

This will be a world earthquake, followed by darkness, that may be felt, while the stars will come down through the darkness, as streaks of light; the moon appearing as a great blood spot in the heavens. And the sea and waves will roar, perhaps as they never did before. And men's hearts will fail them for fear.

At the coming of our Lord He will raise the bodies of all the saints who have lived upon the earth; and immediately following that resurrection, all persons living on earth, who are fit for heaven, ready to meet their Lord and be immediately transferred to the heavenly kingdom, will be changed. "In a moment, in the twinkling of an eye, at the last trumpet; for the trumpet shall sound, and the dead shall be raised incorruptible, and we shall be changed." I Cor. 15:52.

This resurrection will come during the Anti-Christ war, leaving all the foolish virgins, backslidden Christians, to go through this great tribulation, or rather to die in it, for I find only 144,000 who will go through it.

After the Anti-Christ is seated on the Devil's throne, Rev. 13:2, "And the dragon gave him [the Anti-Christ] his power and his throne, and great authority." The Anti-Christ will make war with the saints, the foolish virgins, backslidden Christians, who, finding that the resurrection has taken place, and the wise virgins have been taken up to God, have repented, and amidst war, famine and pestilence, and persecution most terrific, have wept their way back to God. And they will refuse to worship the

Anti-Christ. But the Anti-Christ will overcome them. Rev. 13:7.

All the above saints, who will not receive the mark of the beast upon their foreheads and upon their hand, and will not worship the beast nor his image, will be beheaded. Rev. 20:4.

If this is the Anti-Christ war, "This generation shall not pass, till all these things be fulfilled." Matt. 24:34.

And none of the wicked shall understand; but the wise shall understand. Dan. 12:10.

"Therefore, be ye also ready; for in such an hour as ye think not the Son of Man cometh." Matt. 24:44.

Mr. Taft Wants a New Alliance Policy

On the 14th day of June, 1915, the following notice was printed in many of the leading dailies in the United States:

NEW YORK, June 14.—William H. Taft is expected to formally advocate a departure by the United States from the Washingtonian policy of no entangling alliances with foreign nations when he addresses the League of Peace conference in Philadelphia this week. The national provisional committee of 113 announced the program for the conference today, as follows:

Former President Taft will announce his plan for an alliance with all the great powers with a view to enforcing peace, at a dinner at the Belleview-Stratford Hotel Wednesday evening. Other speakers will be Hamilton Holt, editor of the Independent; Judge George Gray of Delaware, and Oscar S. Straus, former ambassador to Turkey.

The conference proper opens Thursday morning, the anniversary of the battle of

Bunker Hill, in Independence Hall. Addresses will be made by Theodore Marburg, formerly minister to Belgium; Dr. John Grier Hibben, president of Princeton; James M. Beck and Edward Filene, representing the United States Chamber of Commerce.

Judge Taft will preside at the conference. The proposals he will suggest for consideration include an international court to try all justiciable questions; a council of conciliation for the consideration of non justiciable questions; the use of joint military forces against a signatory beginning hostilities contrary to the terms of the alliance; and the formulation and adoption of a code of international law.

We immediately wrote him the following letter:

Los Angeles, Cal., June 15, 1915.
Hon. William H. Taft,
    Philadelphia, Pa.
Dear Sir:

Permit me to call your attention to the enclosed copy of an article I published last September, and mailed a copy to each of the rulers of the several European Nations, on the 30th day of September, 1914; and also to the President of the United

States, and to Secretary Bryan, and to Secretary Daniels.

In your speech before the Peace League you will pave the way for the formation of the Anti-Christ Confederacy; and advise the United States to lead in its formation. This plan will surely be carried out.

I note the many persons who are now advocating such a Confederacy; but when it is formed, and all cry "Peace and Safety, then sudden destruction shall come upon them, as travail upon a woman with child, and they shall not escape." I Thess. 5:3.

Respectfully,
WILLIAM F. MANLEY

GALAXY OF COMING EVENTS

THREE YEARS OF WAR

THE "Great Sword" in the hand of the man on the "Red horse," Revelation 6:4, has been wielded with might, both day and night for the last three years. Peace is really taken from the earth. All Nations not in this war are preparing to defend themselves against the aggressor.

The war will now spread over one-fourth part of the earth. One-fourth part of the earth implies all of Europe, and two other countries as large as all of Europe. But it is sure to come, and terrible will be the consequences.

Famine

Famine is to follow the war and in conjunction with it, to kill people with hunger, over one-fourth part of the earth. Rev. 6:5-6. This famine is now on, and will increase and intensify as a mighty factor in the destruction of human beings until the end of the war. One year from this time we will begin to know what real famine means.

Men will not serve God; will not worship Him in spirit and in truth. They mouth over words before Him, but their hearts are far from Him. God has now arisen "to shake the heavens and the earth and the sea and all nations." Hag. 2:6-7. "To shake terribly the earth." Isa. 2:10-21.

During this famine, terrible plagues and pestilence will break out, and millions will die all over the one-fourth part of the earth, where the war goes on and the famine rages. Then the beasts of the earth, starving and probably suffering with the same plagues, perhaps hydrophobia seizing them, will turn on men, women and children and destroy them. Rev. 6:8.

There are dreadful days just before us. "Pray always that ye may be accounted worthy to escape all these things that shall come to pass, and to stand before the Son of Man." Luke 21:36.

THE REVELATION OF JESUS CHRIST

"THE Revelation of Jesus Christ, which God gave unto Him, to shew unto His servants things which must shortly come to pass; and He sent and signified it by His angel unto His servant John, who bare record of the word of God, and of the testimony of Jesus Christ, and of all things that he saw." Rev. 1:1-2.

The Revelation, not of John, but of Jesus Christ, of facts which God gave to Him, that He might shew them unto His servants; things, not whims, but things which must shortly come to pass. This is a revelation, not a mystification, not a riddle, not a hidden secret.

Jesus Christ reveals all the following wonderful things, which only God knew, until He gave them to Jesus Christ to be revealed to the holy apostle John, by an angel of God.

John in turn bears witness of the word of God; and of the testimony of Jesus Christ, of all things that he saw.

This, then, is a true revealing of things which must shortly come to pass. Our Lord does not present a mysterious riddle to His servants, and have them guess what it all means.

> Blessed is he that readeth, and they that hear the words of this prophecy, and keep those things which are written therein; for the time is at hand. Rev. 1:3.

There is a blessing pronounced upon each person who reads, and upon each person who hears read, the words of the prophecy of this book; and keeps the things that are written therein.

If this book is a series of mysteries, of dark sayings, of hidden things which no man can understand, why should God pronounce a blessing on the man or woman who reads, or hears read, the words of this prophecy; and how could one keep the things that are written therein, if they cannot be understood?

Our Lord reveals facts, things that will come to pass; every one of them. And He wants us to read what He has given. To believe Him and obey Him, not changing or attempting to change, either by adding to, or taking from, the words of this prophecy.

It is a serious matter to tamper with the words of the prophecy of this book. Hear what God says:

> I testify unto every man that heareth the words of the prophecy of this book, If any man shall add unto them, God shall add unto him the plagues which are written in this book: and if any man shall take away from the words of the book

of this prophecy, God shall take away his part from the tree of life, and out of the Holy City, which are written in this book. Rev. 22:18-19, R. V.

JOHN, TO THE SEVEN CHURCHES

JOHN, to the seven churches which are in Asia: Grace be unto you, and peace from Him which is, and which was, and which is to come; and from the seven Spirits which are before His throne; and from Jesus Christ, who is the faithful witness, and the first begotten of the dead, and the Prince of the Kings of the Earth. Unto Him that loved us, and washed us from our sins in His own blood, and hath made us kings and priests unto God and His Father; to Him be glory and dominion forever and ever. Amen. Rev. 1:4-6.

Grace be unto you, and peace, from Him which is, and which was, and which is to come. "From the Almighty God; and from the seven Spirits that are before His throne, and from Jesus Christ, who is the faithful witness, the first-born of the dead, and the ruler of the kings of the earth."

Here our Lord Jesus is classed with the Almighty, and the seven Spirits that are before the throne of God. One with Deity, sends grace and peace to the children of God in the seven

JOHN, TO THE SEVEN CHURCHES 37

churches. The Lord Jesus Christ is the Ruler of the kings of the earth. He is, "Lord of Lords, and King of Kings." Rev. 17:14. He is the first begotten of the dead and the faithful witness. "Unto Him" (Jesus Christ) "that loved us, and washed us from our sins in His own blood, and hath made us kings and priests unto God and His Father; to Him be glory and dominion forever. Amen."

The bloodwashed from every nation, tribe and tongue on earth are made a kingdom; God's Kingdom. All priests unto God.

> Behold, He cometh with clouds; and every eye shall see him, and they also which pierced him; and all kindreds of the earth shall wail because of Him. Even so, Amen. Rev. 1:7.

He cometh with the clouds. When the Lord Jesus ascended to heaven, a cloud received Him out of their sight; and two angels said to His disciples, "This same Jesus, which is taken up from you into heaven, shall so come in like manner as ye have seen Him go into heaven." Acts 1:11. He will make His first appearance in the clouds, as He was last seen in the clouds. There will be a literal re-appearing of the Lord Jesus. "And every eye shall see Him, and they that pierced Him, and all the tribes of the earth shall mourn over him. Even so. Amen."

This probably refers to the final closing

scene told by our Lord, and recorded in Matt. 25:31-32, when "He shall sit upon the throne of His glory and before Him shall be gathered all nations; and he shall separate them one from another, as a shepherd divideth his sheep from the goats." The soldier who thrust the spear into His side; and all the haters of God, and our Lord, will be there, and shall lament, smite their breasts and mourn because of Him, when they see Him on the throne, Lord of Lords and King of Kings.

"Even so, Amen." This implies that as they mourn over Him, or because of Him, God will say Amen to their mourning.

"I am Alpha and Omega, the beginning and the ending, saith the Lord, which is, and which was, and which is to come, the Almighty." Rev. 1:8.

This Revelation comes not from man, but from the Almighty, who is now ruling in heaven and among men, who was before men were on this earth, and who is to come forth and show His authority and power, closing the scene of man's misrule and sin.

> John, who also am your brother and companion in tribulation, and in the kingdom and patience of Jesus Christ, was in the isle that is called Patmos, for the word of God, and for the testimony of Jesus Christ. Rev. 1:9.

JOHN, TO THE SEVEN CHURCHES

The Apostle John declares himself to be our brother. A brother to all who are born of God, and are partakers of the Divine nature. He also is a partaker with all the saints, in the tribulation that comes to all who live godly in Christ Jesus. He also declares himself one with all who make up the Kingdom of priests heretofore referred to. And patience in Jesus Christ, referring to the completed work of Jesus Christ in our hearts, making us as a weaned child, gentle as Jesus.

He was in the isle that is called Patmos. Banished to this island because of his devotion to Christ, and faithfulness to the word of God. Testifying to the power of Christ to save from sin.

> I was in the Spirit on the Lord's day, and heard behind me a great voice, as of a trumpet, saying, I am Alpha and Omega, the first and the last; and, What thou seest, write in a book, and send it unto the seven church which are in Asia; unto Ephesus, and unto Smyrna, and unto Pergamos, and unto Thyatira, and unto Sardis, and unto Philadelphia, and unto Laodicea. Rev. 1:10-11.

He was in the Spirit on the Lord's day. Not in his spirit; and not in a spirit; but in The Spirit, the Holy Spirit. Many evil spirits have gone out into the world, seducing spirits. We are warned against all of those.

John, being in the Spirit, saw what mortal man could not see, unless he is in the Spirit. John was carried away in the Spirit into a wilderness, and saw a woman sitting upon a scarlet colored beast, that had not yet come into existence. Rev. 17:3.

Paul was carried away in the Spirit, into Paradise, and heard things unlawful to be uttered. II Cor. 12:4.

John was carried away in the Spirit on the Lord's day. This was the day of the week on which the Lord was raised from the dead. This is pre-eminently the Lord's day. And he heard behind him a great voice, as of a trumpet speaking. This was the voice of the glorified Christ, who then appeared to John to give him this Revelation, saying, "I am Alpha and Omega, the first and the last, and, What thou seest, write in a book (that it may be preserved), and send it unto the seven churches which are in Asia." *This Book of Revelation to be sent to each church.*

> And I turned to see the voice that spake with me. And being turned I saw seven golden candlesticks; and in the midst of the seven candlesticks one like unto the Son of Man, clothed with a garment down to the foot, and girt about the paps with a golden girdle. Rev. 1:12-13.

JOHN, TO THE SEVEN CHURCHES

And John turned to see the person speaking to him; and he saw seven golden candlesticks. Only candlesticks. Not lamps, lights, or flaming torches. These candlesticks represented the seven churches. "The seven candlesticks are the seven churches." Rev. 1:20. These candlesticks are golden. Gold in the Scriptures stands for purity and great value. And in the midst of the candlesticks is one like unto the Son of Man. This one is Christ, standing or walking in the midst of His people, in each assembly of believers, as "Head over all things to the church," (Eph. 1:22) clothed with a garment down to the foot and girt about with a golden girdle. The priestly robes and girdle. Jesus Christ is our High Priest.

> His head and his hairs were white like wool, as white as snow, and his eyes were as a flame of fire; and his feet like unto fine brass, as if they burned in a furnace; and his voice as the sound of many waters. Rev. 1:14-15.

Not His hair, only, but His head was white as snow; and His eyes were as a flame of fire, flashing with Divine majesty, and His feet like unto burnished brass, as if it had been refined in a furnace. Glorious in appearance. And His voice as the sound of many waters. Majestic. This is our glorious risen Lord. No more the rejected and despised Galilean, the man of sorrows, with no place to lay His head. He comes forth the Mighty Conqueror, with the keys of death and hell.

"And he had in his right hand seven stars: and out of his mouth went a sharp two-edged sword: and his countenance was as the sun shineth in his strength. And when I saw him I fell at his feet as dead. And he laid his right hand upon me, saying unto me, Fear not: I am the first and the last: I am he that liveth, and was dead; and, behold, I am alive for evermore, Amen; and have the keys of hell and of death." Rev. 1:16-18.

He had in his right hand seven stars. These stars represent the Pastors of the seven churches, or assemblies, upheld, directed and protected by their risen and glorified Lord. "The seven stars are the seven angels of the seven churches." Rev. 1:20. Not literal angels of God, or spiritual beings, as we discover from Rev. 2:1, 8, 12, 18, and Rev. 3:1, 7, 14. In each of these seven commands, the Apostle John was ordered to write to the angel of the church. John could not write to an angel proper, or to a spiritual or heavenly being; but to the minister, or pastor over that particular church or assembly. The pastor in the hand of his Lord, is here called an angel.

Out of His mouth proceeded a sharp, two-edged sword; and His countenance was as the sun shineth in his strength. What a wonder-

JOHN, TO THE SEVEN CHURCHES 43

ful description of our glorified human, Divine, risen Lord, as He appeared to John on Patmos. He carries no weapon but the word of His mouth. He speaks and it is done. His word is sharper than a two-edged sword.

When John saw Him, he fell at his feet as one dead. The presence of such glory; the Majesty of His Divine person, was more than the body of the sainted John could endure; and so he fell as one dead.

"And He laid His right hand upon me, saying, Fear not: I am the first and the last, and the living one; and I was dead, and behold I am alive forevermore, and have the keys of death and hades." R. V.

John, strengthened by the divine touch of his Lord, hears these soothing, wonderful words. The Speaker is the first of all things in the universe. All things were made by Him. "He laid the foundation of the earth and the heavens are the works of His hands." Heb. 1:10. "But made Himself of no reputation, and took upon him the form of a servant, and was made in the likeness of men; and being found in fashion as a man, He humbled Himself, and became obedient unto death, even the death of the cross." Phil. 2:7, 8. He was dead, and, behold, He is not dead, but alive forevermore, and has the keys and controls both death and hell. And as the risen conqueror of Satan, death, and hell, He commands John to write this Book of Revelation.

> Write the things which thou hast seen, and the things which are, and the things which shall be hereafter: The mystery of the seven stars which thou sawest in my right hand, and the seven golden candlesticks. The seven stars are the angels of the seven churches; and the seven candlesticks which thou sawest are the seven churches. Rev. 1:19-20.

Write, therefore. The things which have been shown him, and the things which are now before him; and all the things that shall be shown unto him. The mystery of the seven stars which thou sawest in my right hand, and the seven golden candlesticks. Our Lord is revealing hidden things to John, and because these candlesticks, and the stars, are not to be taken literally, He reveals their meaning, saying, The seven stars are the angels of the seven churches; and the seven candlesticks are the seven churches.

An individual church or assembly is here represented by a candlestick, which of itself has no light and can give none, but is intended to bear or hold a candle, lamp, or burning torch, that will shed light on all around. God is light, Christ is the light of the world, because He is God. And without Him we are all darkness, and can do nothing. We must have Christ and God in us, as the candle is in the candlestick. When, "Filled with all the fullness of God," Eph. 3:19, we become the "Light of the world; and the salt of the earth." Matt. 5:13-14.

THE KINGDOM OF HEAVEN

AND in the days of these kings shall the God of Heaven set up a kingdom, which shall never be destroyed and the kingdom shall not be left to other people, but it shall break in pieces and consume all these kingdoms, and it shall stand forever. Forasmuch as thou sawest that the stone was cut out of the mountain without hands, and that it break in pieces the iron, the brass, the clay, the silver, and the gold; the great God hath made known to the king what shall come to pass hereafter; and the dream is certain, and the interpretation thereof sure. Dan. 2:44-45.

Here God reveals to Nebuchadnezzar a series of consequences, after which the God of Heaven will set up a kingdom that shall stand forever. And this Kingdom of God will pulverize, and utterly destroy, all other kingdoms.

Why do the heathen rage, and the people imagine a vain thing? The kings of the earth set themselves, and the rulers take counsel together, against the Lord, and against His annointed, saying, Let

THE KINGDOM OF HEAVEN 47

us break their bands asunder, and cast away their cords from us. He that sitteth in the heavens shall laugh; the Lord shall have them in derision. Then shall He speak unto them in His wrath, and vex them in his sore displeasure. Yet have I set my king upon my holy hill of Zion. I will declare the decree: the Lord hath said unto me, Thou art my Son; this day have I begotten thee. Ask of me, and I shall give thee the heathen for thine inheritance, and the utmost parts of the earth for thy possession. Thou shalt break them with a rod of iron; thou shalt dash them in pieces like a potter's vessel. Be wise now, therefore, O ye kings: be instructed, ye judges of the earth. Serve the Lord with fear and rejoice with trembling. Kiss the Son, lest He be angry, and ye perish from the way, when His wrath is kindled but a little. Blessed are all they that put their trust in Him. Psa. 2.

The Son of God is to be the king and ruler of the whole earth. God will set His Son upon the throne of David, in Jerusalem, and He shall break the kings and kingdoms of this earth with a rod of iron; and dash them to pieces like a potter's vessel. Man's rule shall come to an end; and God shall rule forever, and His kingdom shall fill the whole earth. These things are to come to pass in "The time of the end." Dan. 12:9-13.

Of the increase of His government and peace there shall be no end, upon the throne of David, and upon His kingdom [in Jerusalem, and over the twelve tribes of Israel], to order it, and to establish it, with judgment and with justice from henceforth even forever. The zeal of the Lord of Hosts will perform this. Isa. 9:7.

And I will set up one shepherd over them, and he shall feed them, even my servant David; he shall feed them, and he shall be their shepherd. And I, the Lord, will be their God, and my servant David a prince among them; I the Lord have spoken it. Ezek. 34:23-24.

Isaiah and Ezekiel prophesied three hundred years after the death of David. So this prophecy could not refer to him; but it does refer to David's son, who would sit on David's throne in Jerusalem, and reign over all the earth.

And He said unto them, How say they that Christ is David's son? And David himself saith in the Book of Psalms, The Lord said unto my Lord, Sit thou on my right hand, till I make thine enemies thy

THE KINGDOM OF HEAVEN 49

footstool. David therefore calleth him Lord, how is he then his son? Luke 20:41-44.

The Jews could not answer this question; but they knew that Jesus quoted the Scriptures correctly, that Christ is David's son.

In Rev. 22:16, Jesus Christ declares, "I, Jesus, have sent mine angel to testify unto you these things in the churches; I am the root and the offspring of David."

He is the prince of the kings of the earth. He is the true heir to every throne on earth. And he will sit on David's throne in Jerusalem and reign over all, for a thousand years.

> I saw in the night visions, and, behold, one like the Son of Man came with the clouds of heaven, and came to the ancient of days, and they brought Him near before Him. And there was given Him dominion, and glory, and a kingdom, that all people, nations, and languages, should serve Him: His dominion is an everlasting dominion, which shall not pass away, and His kingdom that which shall not be destroyed. Dan. 7:13, 14.

Afterward shall the children of Israel return and seek the Lord their God, and David their king; and shall fear the Lord and His goodness in the latter days. Hosea, 3:5.

All of this takes place in the latter days. At the end of the "Times of the Gentiles." Luke 21:24. When the Gentiles are cut off; and a remnant of Israel is grafted into the true olive tree. Jesus Christ is the central figure throughout the Book of Revelation. We see Him in Majestic glory in the first chapter. We find Him overseeing the churches; commending the good, condemning the wrong, and directing all, in the second and third chapters. We see Him with all the resurrected saints in heaven, in the seventh chapter; and opening the last seal in the eighth chapter. And great rejoicing in heaven because the kingdoms of this world have become the kingdoms of our Lord, and of His Christ, in the eleventh chapter, fifteenth verse; and we find Him the central figure in the tenth and eleventh verses of the twelfth chapter. We find Him with the first fruits of the resurrection, 144,000 in number, on Mount Sion, in the fourteenth chapter. We find him in the sixteenth chapter, fifteenth verse, saying, "Behold, I come as a thief. Blessed is he that watcheth, and keepeth his garments, lest he walk naked, and they see his shame."

We find the beast making war with the Lamb, in the seventeenth chapter. And in the nineteenth chapter, the marriage of the Lamb takes place and the Lord Jesus, with all the saints and angels ride on white horses, going forth

THE KINGDOM OF HEAVEN 51

to make war; and to destroy the Anti-Christ and his army. In the twentieth chapter, Satan is chained and cast into the bottomless pit, and Jesus Christ raises all persons who have ever lived on this earth and have not been heretofore resurrected; and, sitting on the great white throne, He judges them. The return of Christ to this earth is the subject under consideration all through the book. Heaven, earth, and hell are brought in as they relate to His coming. Most of the scenes occur on earth; but the things that occur, have their origin in heaven. God speaks from the throne; and the earth quakes.

The devil that deceived them was cast into the lake of fire and brimstone, where the beast and the false prophet were cast, a thousand years before.

KEY TO THE BOOK OF REVELATION

THERE are seven seals to be opened, and seven trumpets to be sounded, and seven thunders to utter their voices, and seven last plagues to be poured out. Each coming in their proper order, as revealed in this book.

This book being a panorama of things that will surely occur, or come to pass, the reader must continually keep in mind the things that have already transpired; and the condition of the world under which he is then studying.

There are seven seals to be opened, and at the opening of each seal certain things occur, entirely different from all other occurrences. These occurrences come in the order given in the Book of Revelation. The occurrences under the opening of each seal cannot come until that seal is opened. All the occurrences under the opening of the seven seals will have taken place before the first of the seven trumpets will be sounded. And under the sounding of the other trumpets, distinct and entirely different things come to pass.

After the sounding of the sixth trumpet, seven thunders utter their voices. Those thunders will not come until six trumpets have been sounded. And the seventh trumpet will not be sounded until after the seven thunders have uttered their voices. And all of these will have come, and gone, before the first of the seven last plagues is poured out, and each plague will bring new scenes before us.

We find order in all the works of God, and now that He is revealing to us the things which must come to pass, we should not expect that He would present them in a maze of confusion, but in perfect order. Remember that God is revealing facts, not fiction; so clearly stated, that He will not suffer any change to be made in them.

THE BOOK OF REVELATION

HE Book of Revelation commences with these words: "The Revelation of Jesus Christ, which God gave Him, to show unto His servants things which must shortly come to pass."

A series of things which must come to pass in connection with the coming, or revealing of the Lord Jesus Christ. Mighty things shall transpire. The Devil shall be cast out, and imprisoned. The wicked shall be defeated. The earth shall be cleansed. Christ shall be vindicated. The sons of God shall be gloriously liberated, and glorified with Christ; and the restoration of all earthly creatures and conditions shall be complete; and God shall be glorified in all.

The Revelation, or revealing of Jesus Christ in His return to earth, giving the things that must take place, in the order in which they will take place, in connection with His return.

The book is a panorama of the things seen; and a faithful statement of words and sounds heard by the holy Apostle John. All concerning Jesus Christ, and His return to earth to claim His own, and to bring them into the resurrection life and spiritual realm in which God and angels are; making their material bodies spiritual bodies, with faculties and powers enabling them to stand in the presence of God, seeing His face, and comprehending heavenly things, and conditions as they are. In this spiritual and heavenly condition, we shall reign with Christ, on this restored earth, for a thousand years. This is the Sabbath of the Lord.

The first declaration in this book after its introduction is, "Behold He cometh with clouds and every eye shall see Him; and all kindreds of the earth shall wail because of Him, Even so, Amen." And the concluding words of this book, from the Lord Himself, are, "Surely, I come quickly."

The things heard and seen, that are herein recorded, were so correctly presented to John, and clearly stated, that not one word may be changed; and a great curse is pronounced against any person who adds to, or takes from, the words of the prophecy of this book. No such warning is appended to any other book in the Bible. We believe that great confusion has come to God's children by taking from, and adding to, the words of this prophecy.

Let us study this book very carefully, and observe very closely what God says.

The Book of Revelation seems to be the last book in the sacred volume given to the church. This being a fact, we must study it in connection with what our Lord said about His return to this earth, recorded in John 14: 2, 3, and in connection with all other Scriptures on this subject.

> In my Father's house are many mansions: if it were not so, I would have told you. I go to prepare a place for you. And if I go and prepare a place for you, I will come again, and receive you unto myself; that where I am, there ye may be also. John 14: 2, 3.

The return of our Lord to take us to His Father's Home is mentioned hundreds of times in the Bible, and is the brightest star in all our constellation. If the Book of Revelation is really a revelation of things in connection with His return to this earth, then we will find the proof of that fact in this book.

The Lord Jesus gave the apostles a clear statement of the signs of His coming back to earth, in the twenty-fourth chapter of Matthew, in the thirteenth chapter of Mark, and in the twenty-first chapter of Luke. As Jesus and His disciples passed out of the temple, they called His attention to the buildings and great stones, and Jesus answered: "See ye not all these things? Verily I say unto you, There shall not be left here one stone upon another, that shall not be thrown down." Matt. 24:2.

> And as He sat upon the Mount of Olives, over against the temple, Peter and James and John and Andrew asked him

THE BOOK OF REVELATION 57

privately, Tell us, when shall these things be? and what shall be the sign of Thy coming, and of the end of the world? And Jesus answered and said unto them, Take heed that no man deceive you. For many shall come in my name, saying, I am Christ; and shall deceive many. Matt. 24:3-5.

Go ye not, therefore, after them. But when ye shall hear of wars and commotions, be not terrified: for these things must first come to pass; but the end is not by and by. Then said He unto them, Nation shall rise against nation, and kingdom against kingdom: and great earthquakes shall be in divers places, and famines, and pestilences; and fearful sights and great signs shall there be from heaven. But before all these, they shall lay their hands on you, and persecute you, delivering you up to the synagogues and into prisons, being brought before kings and rulers for my name's sake. And it shall turn to you for a testimony. Settle it therefore in your hearts, not to mediate before what ye shall answer: for I will give you a mouth and wisdom, which all your adversaries shall not be able to gainsay nor resist. And ye shall be hated of all men for my name's sake. But there shall not an hair of your head perish. In your patience possess ye your souls. And when ye shall see Jerusalem compassed with armies, then know that the desolation thereof is nigh. Then let them which are in Judea flee to the mountains; and let them which are in the midst of it depart out; and let not them that are in the countries enter thereinto. For these be the days of vengeance, that all things which are written may be fulfilled. But woe unto them that are with child, and to them that give suck, in those days, for there shall be great distress in the land, and wrath upon this people. And they shall fall by the edge of the sword, and shall be led away captive into all nations: and Jerusalem shall be trodden down of the Gentiles, until the times of the Gentiles be fulfilled. Luke 21:8-24.

This Scripture covers the destruction of Jerusalem, and the curse that fell on the Jews and their land, down to this day. This is the answer of our Lord to the question asked, "When shall these things be?" referring to His declaration that, "Not one stone shall be left that shall not be thrown down."

All this Scripture has been literally fulfilled. Read Josephus' description of the destruction of Jerusalem, and the history of the Jews down to the present time, and you will see how accurately Christ foretold it all.

THE SIGNS OF HIS COMING

NOW we come to the second question, concerning the return of our Lord. "Tell us, what shall be the sign of Thy coming." The destruction of Jerusalem, and the wars, pestilences, famines, fearful sights and signs since then, are not the signs of His coming. What are the signs of His coming? Our Lord answers this question in Matthew 24:23, and in Mark 13:21, and in Luke, 21:25.

> Then if any man shall say unto you, Lo, here is Christ, or there; believe it not. For there shall arise false Christs, and false prophets, and shall shew great signs and wonders; insomuch that, if it were possible, they shall deceive the very elect. Behold, I have told you before. Wherefore, if they shall say unto you, Behold, He is in the desert, go not forth: behold, He is in the secret chambers; believe it not. For as the lightning cometh out of the east, and shineth even unto the west, so shall also the coming of the Son of Man be. * * * Immediately after the tribulation of those days shall the sun be darkened, and the moon shall not give her

light, and the stars shall fall from heaven, and the powers of the heavens shall be shaken: and then shall appear the sign of the Son of Man in heaven: and then shall all the tribes of the earth mourn, and they shall see the Son of Man coming in the clouds of heaven with power and great glory. And He shall send His angels with a great sound of a trumpet, and they shall gather together His elect from the four winds, from one end of heaven to the other. Now learn a parable of the fig tree: When his branch is yet tender, and putteth forth leaves, ye know that summer is nigh. Matt. 24:23-32.

And when these things begin to come to pass, then look up, and lift up your heads; for your redemption draweth nigh. And He spake to them a parable: Behold the fig tree, and all the trees: When they now shoot forth, ye see and know of your own selves that summer is now nigh at hand. So likewise ye, when ye see these things come to pass, know ye that the Kingdom of God is nigh at hand. Verily I say unto you, This generation shall not pass away till all be fulfilled. Heaven and earth shall pass away: but my words shall not pass away. Luke 21:28-33.

As the leaves coming forth in the springtime on the fig tree, and all the trees, indicate

THE SIGNS OF HIS COMING 61

winter is past, and the spring is present, and the summer is near: so the three signs here given indicate that the Lord Jesus is at the door, to raise the dead, and translate the living saints; and to set up His kingdom upon earth for a thousand years.

And our Lord tells us that when the first sign appears, that is the darkness, thick darkness, to lift up your heads, for your redemption draweth nigh. And when all three signs have been seen by us, to know that it, the Kingdom of God, is at the door, that Christ may then appear any minute.

These signs come immediately after the tribulations of those days. The world will have been in tribulation just before these signs appear, and all of these signs will come in conjunction, one with the other, as given by our Lord. The generation then living will see all the signs; and will not pass away until Jesus Christ comes, and raises the righteous dead and translates the righteous living, taking them up into heaven; and until the Anti-Christ has finished his reign of destruction and blasphemy. Then the Lord will return to this earth, bringing the saints with Him, to destroy all people who have taken the mark of the beast, or Anti-Christ. And the Anti-Christ and the False Prophet will be cast alive into the lake of fire and brimstone; and Satan will be bound and shut up in the bottomless pit for one thousand years; and the Lord Jesus, who is the Prince of the Kings of the Earth, shall reign over the whole earth during the thousand years.

This will be the Sabbath of the Lord: For the "earth shall be full of the knowledge of the Lord, as the waters cover the sea." Isa. 11:9.

If the Book of Revelation is a panorama of the occurrences before, at, and after, the coming of Christ, we will find the signs of His coming, as He gave them to the disciples. And we will also find them in their proper place in relation to all other scenes and phenomena.

> And I beheld when he had opened the sixth seal, and lo, there was a great earthquake; and the sun became black as sackcloth of hair, and the moon became as blood: And the stars of heaven fell unto the earth, even as a fig tree casteth her untimely figs, when she is shaken of a mighty wind. And the heavens parted as a scroll when it is rolled together: and every mountain and island were moved out of their places. Rev. 6:12-14.

Here are all the signs given by our Lord Jesus Christ to the disciples, and in conjunction, one after the other; and in the same order that Christ gave them. And coming in conjunction with a world earthquake, that will move every mountain and island out of their

THE SIGNS OF HIS COMING 63

places, and causing consternation throughout the whole world.

"And the kings of the earth, and the great men and the rich men, and the chief captains, and the mighty men, and every bondman, and every free man, hid themselves in the dens and in the rocks of the mountains; and said to the mountains and rocks, Fall on us, and hide us from the face of Him that sitteth on the throne, and from the wrath of the Lamb: for the great day of His wrath is come; and who shall be able to stand? Rev. 6:15-17.

The signs all being present, or having occurred, indicate that Christ is at the door, to raise the dead. The whole world is thrown into terror, and cry out for rocks to fall on them. Now we have a fact established: Jesus Christ will come when the sixth seal is opened. Not before, not later. This world earthquake will usher in the signs of His coming. All fairly well-informed people know that such an earthquake, world-wide, moving every mountain and island out of their places, followed by the sun becoming black as sackcloth of hair, and the moon appearing as blood, and the stars falling to the earth, has not taken place since the Book of Revelation was given. But it will take place, and come as accurately as the destruction of Jerusalem came. And when it does come, Jesus Christ will be at the door to raise the dead, and catch the saints away.

And as we have borne the image of the earthy, we shall also bear the image of the heavenly. Now this I say, brethren, that flesh and blood cannot inherit the Kingdom of God; neither doth corruption inherit incorruption. Behold, I shew you a mystery: We shall not all sleep, but we shall all be changed, in a moment, in the twinkling of an eye, at the last trump: for the trumpet shall sound, and the dead shall be raised incorruptible, and we shall be changed. For this corruptible must put on incorruption, and this mortal must put on immortality. So when this corruptible shall have put on incorruption, and this mortal shall have put on immortality, then shall be brought to pass the saying that is written, Death is swallowed up in victory. O death, where is thy sting? O grave, where is thy victory? I Cor. 15:49-55.

For the Lord Himself shall descend from heaven with a shout, with the voice of the archangel, and with the trump of God: and the dead in Christ shall rise first: then we which are alive and remain shall be caught up together with them in the clouds, to meet the Lord in the air; and so shall we ever be with the Lord. Wherefore comfort one another with these words. I Thes. 4:16, 18.

THE SIGNS OF HIS COMING 65

> I tell you, in that night there shall be two men in one bed; the one shall be taken, and the other shall be left. Two women shall be grinding together; the one shall be taken, and the other left. Two men shall be in the field; the one shall be taken, and the other left. Luke 17:34-36.

In these three Scriptures we have the resurrection clearly stated, taking place at the coming of the Lord Jesus to gather the saints unto Himself, as set forth in II Thes. 2:1.

When the sixth seal is opened, God will shake terribly the earth.

> And they shall go into the holes of the rocks, and into the caves of the earth, for fear of the Lord, and for the glory of His majesty, when He ariseth to shake terribly the earth. In that day a man shall cast his idols of silver, and his idols of gold, which they made each one for himself to worship, to the moles and to the bats; to go into the clefts of the rocks, and into the tops of the ragged rocks, for fear of the Lord, and for the glory of His majesty, when He ariseth to shake terribly the earth. Isa. 2:19-21.

And the sun will become black as sackcloth of hair, and the moon will become as blood, and the stars will fall unto the earth. This is all positively stated by the Lord Himself. And the resurrection will then take place.

> And I saw another angel ascending from the east, having the seal of the living God: and he cried with a loud voice to the four angels, to whom it was given to hurt the earth and the sea, saying, Hurt not the earth, neither the sea, nor the trees, till we have sealed the servants of our God in their foreheads. And I heard the number of them which were sealed: and there were sealed a hundred and forty and four thousand of all the tribes of the children of Israel. Of the tribe of Juda were sealed twelve thousand. Of the tribe of Reuben were sealed twelve thousand. Of the tribe of Gad were sealed twelve thousand. Of the tribe of Aser were sealed twelve thousand. Of the tribe of Nephthalim were sealed twelve thousand. Of the tribe of Manasses were sealed twelve thouasnd. Of the tribe of Simeon were sealed twelve thousand. Of the tribe of Levi were sealed twelve thousand. Of the tribe of Issachar were sealed twelve thousand. Of the tribe of Zabulon were sealed twelve thousand. Of the tribe of Benjamin were sealed twelve thousand. Of the tribe of Joseph were sealed twelve thousand. Rev. 7:2-8.

And then after this sealing of the 144,000:

<small>First Resurrection</small>

After this I beheld, and, lo, a great multitude, which no man could number, of all nations, and kindreds, and people, and tongues, stood before the throne, and before the Lamb, clothed with white robes, and palms in their hands; and cried with a loud voice, saying, Salvation to our God which sitteth upon the throne, and unto the Lamb. And all the angels stood round about the throne, and about the elders and the four beasts, and fell before the throne on their faces, and worshipped God, saying, Amen: Blessing, and glory, and wisdom, and thanksgiving, and honour, and power, and might, be unto our God forever and ever. Amen. And one of the elders answered, saying unto me, What are these which are arrayed in white robes, and whence came they? And I said unto him, Sir, thou knowest. And he said to me, These are they which came out of great tribulation, and have washed their robes, and made them white in the blood of the Lamb. Therefore are they before the throne of God, and serve Him day and night in His temple: and He that sitteth on the throne shall dwell among them.

They shall hunger no more, neither thirst any more; neither shall the sun light on them, nor any heat: for the Lamb which is in the midst of the throne shall feed them and shall lead them unto living fountains of waters, and God shall wipe all tears from their eyes. Rev. 7:9-17.

Here we have the positive statement that these are the resurrected saints from all nations, kindreds, peoples and tongues, having washed their robes in the Blood of the Lamb; and having come up out of great tribulation. Therefore, because they have washed their robes in the Blood of the Lamb, and have come out of great tribulation, they are now off of the earth, and out of their earthly conditions; and are before the throne of God in heaven, to serve Him day and night in His temple, and God Himself shall dwell among them, and the Lamb which is in the midst shall feed them, and shall lead them unto living fountains of waters, and God shall wipe away all tears from their eyes.

While the fifth angel was sealing the 144,000 on earth, the Lord Jesus, as a thief in the night, according to His own word, and according to I Thes. 5:2, and suddenly, "In the twinkling of an eye," changes the living saints, as set forth in I Cor. 15:52; and catches them up to be forever with the Lord, as also set forth in I Thes. 4:17.

THE SIGNS OF HIS COMING 69

Observe, all of this comes under the opening of the sixth seal. The seventh seal has not been opened yet; and five seals had been opened before the sixth seal was opened; and under the opening of each seal, tremendous things occur, in heaven, on earth, or in hell. All of these are stirred because of what God is doing.

This scene in heaven has brought all the angels together, surrounding the throne, and the elders and the living creatures, because of the occurrence that has just taken place; the home-coming of all the resurrected children of God, in their glorified state, with their shining faces. The Blood-washed sons of God, at Home, and all the angels present. They hear the saints crying out, "Salvation to our God, which sitteth on the throne, and unto the Lamb." Referring to their own salvation, their purification, their elevation from sin to sonship, sons of God, by the Blood of the Lamb. And the angels fell before the throne on their faces, and worshiped God, saying, "Amen." This amen, was amen to what the saints had said.

This scene is a Jubilee in heaven over the home-coming of the Blood-washed throng. All the saints are here from all nations, and kindred and people, and tongues; and all the angels, too; all worshipping God and the Lamb. The saints are not yet crowned, for the wedding supper of the Lamb has not yet taken place. That comes in the nineteenth chapter of Revelation. The coming of Jesus Christ is definitely fixed, to take place at the opening of the sixth seal. If we will carefully consider what things come to pass on the opening of the first, second, third, fourth and fifth seals, we may discover where we now are, in relation to the coming of our Lord.

JOHN CAUGHT UP INTO HEAVEN

AFTER this I looked, and, behold, a door was opened in heaven and the first voice which I heard was as it were of a trumpet talking with me; which said, Come up hither, and I will shew thee things which must be hereafter. And immediately I was in the Spirit: and, behold, a throne was set in heaven and one sat on the throne. And he that sat was to look upon like a jasper and a sardine stone: and there was a rainbow round about the throne, in sight like unto an emerald. Rev. 4:1-3.

After John had written in a book the messages for the seven churches in Asia, recorded in the second and third chapters of Revelation, he looked and saw a door opened in heaven; an opening through the clouds, enabling him to see beyond earthly things. And he heard a voice as of a trumpet speaking to him; the same voice that he heard when on Patmos, on the Lord's day. Rev. 1:10. The voice of the Lord Jesus Christ. The voice that reaches and thrills the soul, saying, Come up hither and I will shew thee things which must come to pass hereafter. Up into heaven where Jesus Christ is, and He, Jesus Christ, will show John things, the very things that must come to pass hereafter. Not phantoms, or symbols or myths, but realities; things that must come to pass.

Straightway (immediately) I was in the Spirit, as he was on the Lord's day, in Patmos, and being in the Spirit he could hear spiritual things and see spiritual beings. In this state he was caught up into heaven; not in body, for flesh and blood could not be caught up into heaven, but his soul and spirit could be. The Lord had said unto him, Come up hither, and the power that commanded him, caught him up into heaven, where he saw the throne of God, and One sitting upon the throne. This one is God, sitting upon His throne. And He that sat was to look upon like a jasper and a sardine stone. Jasper is a precious stone of various colors, as purple, blue, green. The New Jerusalem, in heaven, is said to have light like a jasper stone, clear as crystal (Rev. 21:11); and a sardine stone is a bright red color.

The prophet Ezekiel was permitted to see the Lord on His throne, and he said:

> And I saw as the color of amber, as the appearance of fire round about within it from the appearance of his loins even upward, and from the appearance of his loins even downward, I saw as it were the

JOHN CAUGHT UP INTO HEAVEN 73

appearance of fire, and it had brightness round about. As the appearance of the bow that is in the cloud in the day of rain, so was the appearance of the brightness round about. This was the appearance of the likeness of the glory of the Lord. And when I saw it, I fell upon my face, and I heard a voice of one that spake. Ezek. 1:27-28.

Twenty-four Thrones

The rainbow around the throne was like an emerald. A soft green color. "And round about the throne were four and twenty seats [thrones, R. V.], and upon the seats I saw four and twenty elders sitting, clothed in white raiment; and they had on their heads crowns of gold. And out of the throne proceeded lightnings and thunderings and voices: and there were seven lamps of fire burning before the throne, which are the seven spirits of God." Rev. 4:4, 5.

And these four and twenty thrones were occupied at that time by four and twenty elders arrayed in white garments; and on their heads were crowns of gold. We find in chapter five, eighth verse, that these elders had each one of them a harp, and golden vials full of incense, which are the prayers of the saints. There is good reason to believe that these elders were glorified saints, crowned and robed and enthroned, with harp in hand praising God for their salvation.

> And I John saw these things, and heard them. And when I had heard and seen, I fell down to worship before the feet of the angel which shewed me these things. Then saith he unto me, See thou do it not; for I am thy fellow servant, and of thy brethren the prophets, and of them which keep the sayings of this book: worship God. Rev. 22:8, 9.

John supposed this angel was God, because of his glorious appearance, and fell down at his feet to worship him. "Then said he unto me, see thou do it not: for I am thy fellow servant, and of thy brethren the prophets, and of them which keep the sayings of this book: worship God." Here we find a human being glorified; and in the likeness of God: so John thought he was God. And this resurrected human being, now glorified, is sent by the Lord Jesus to show John the things that must come to pass. But how came this person and the twenty-four elders to be in heaven, when John was caught up, about the year A. D. 96? *Answer:*

Because, "The graves were opened and many bodies of the saints which slept arose, and came out of the graves after His resurrection, and went into the holy city, and appeared unto many." Matt. 27:52, 53.

JOHN CAUGHT UP INTO HEAVEN

These saints who came out of their graves after Jesus arose, are, along with Christ "Firstfruits" of the resurrection.

> For as in Adam all die, even so in Christ shall all be made alive. But every man in his own order: Christ the first-fruits; afterward, they that are Christ's at His coming. Then cometh the end, when He shall have delivered up the kingdom to God, even the Father; when He shall have put down all rule and all authority and power. I Cor. 15: 22-24.

Here are the three orders of the resurrection. First Christ and the many bodies of the saints that had fallen asleep, who came out of their graves after Him. These are the first-fruits of the resurrection, or the first order or company to enter into the glorified resurrection life with God.

Second Order: "They that are Christ's at His coming." These are the second order, or company that will be raised when Jesus comes. "Then cometh the end," or the third order or company, when all the remaining dead will be raised. Rev. 20:13. Further proof is found in Rev. 14:1-4, as follows:

The First Fruits

> And I looked, and, lo, a Lamb stood on the mount Zion, and with him a hundred forty and four thousand, having his Fath-

er's name written in their foreheads. And I heard a voice from heaven, as the voice of many waters, and as the voice of a great thunder: and I heard the voice of harpers harping with their harps: and they sung as it were a new song before the throne, and before the four beasts [living creatures, R.V.], and the elders: and no man could learn that song but the hundred and forty and four thousand, which were redeemed from the earth. These are they which were not defiled with women; for they are virgins. These are they which follow the Lamb whithersoever he goeth. These were redeemed from among men, being the first-fruits unto God and to the Lamb.

This company who were resurrected when Jesus came forth conqueror over death and hell, and who have been with Him, following the Lamb whithersoever He goeth, can sing a song that no other saint can sing. Jesus Christ is our High Priest; and as such He took those resurrected saints, the first-fruits, the wave sheaf; and presented them to God, a wave offering, the First-fruits of the great harvest of saints that will be gathered home when our Lord shall reappear.

Now we see clearly why John found the twenty-four elders; and the one who showed him the things that must shortly come to pass, already crowned and on thrones in heaven, wearing their white robes with harp in hand.

And out of the throne proceeded lightnings and voices and thunders, indicating the awful Majesty and power of God. Moses feared and quaked when he saw and heard the lightning flash and the thunder roar, on Sinai.

"And there were seven lamps of fire burning before the throne, which are the seven Spirits of God." Our God is a consuming fire to the wicked, who continue impenitent. These seven flames of fire indicate God in His fullness.

> And before the throne there was a sea of glass like unto crystal: and in the midst of the throne, and round about the throne, were four beasts full of eyes before and behind. And the first beast was like a lion, and the second beast like a calf, and the third beast had a face as a man, and the fourth beast was like a flying eagle. And the four beasts had each of them six wings about him; and they were full of eyes within: and they rest not day and night, saying, Holy, holy, holy, Lord God Almighty, which was, and is, and is to come. Rev. 4:6-8.

And before the throne, as it were, a sea of glass, like unto crystal. Not glass in fact; but it had the appearance of glass; clear and beautiful as crystal; wonderfully grand and glorious to behold.

And round about the throne, in the midst of the throne, were four living creatures full of eyes before and behind. The prophet Ezekiel saw and described four living creatures quite similar to these. See Ezek. 1:4-28. Read this description, it is very wonderful.

The prophet Isaiah saw and described the seraphim in the presence of the Lord sitting on His throne. "Above it stood the seraphim: each one had six wings; with twain he covered his face, and with twain he covered his feet, and with twain he did fly. And one cried unto another, and said, Holy, holy, holy, is the Lord of hosts: the whole earth is full of his glory. And the posts of the door moved at the voice of him that cried, and the house was filled with smoke." Isa. 6:2-4.

This was seven hundred and sixty years before Christ appeared on earth. Those seraphim could not be redeemed, resurrected human beings for no human being had been resurrected at that time. Neither could they be resurrected until our Lord had arisen from the dead. He is the first-fruits of them that slept.

Those seraphim have six wings; and four faces, similar to the living creatures in Rev. 4:6-8. The living creatures in Rev. 4:6-8 were flying "In the midst of the throne, and round about the throne." And the seraphim Isaiah saw "Stood above the throne." Isa. 6:2. Those could not be human beings flying or standing in or above the throne of God.

JOHN CAUGHT UP INTO HEAVEN 79

We believe all these descriptions refer to the same living creatures and that these living creatures are heavenly beings, and not human beings. There is nothing in their appearance or description, or actions, indicating that they are glorified human beings. On the contrary, at their initiative the twenty-four elders fell down before God, and worshipped Him. These living creatures are constantly on the move, in and around the throne, crying, Holy, holy, holy, is the Lord God, the Almighty.

> And when the living creatures give glory and honour and thanks to him that sat on the throne, who liveth forever and ever, the four and twenty elders fall down before him that sat on the throne, and worship him that liveth forever and ever, and cast their crowns before the throne, saying, Thou art worthy, O Lord, to receive glory and honour and power: for thou hast created all things, and for thy pleasure they are and were created. Rev. 4:9-11.

The living creatures, although so closely connected with the throne, were not crowned. Crowns are only for the children of God, persons who have been born of God, made partakers of the Divine nature. Heirs of God, and joint heirs with Christ. The elders were crowned, showing that they were resurrected, glorified human beings. There is no mention in the Bible of any of the heavenly host wearing crowns, except God; and His children. Men and women who, having been born of God, are sons. Not bastards, but sons of God. They will wear crowns.

A BOOK WITH SEVEN SEALS

AND I saw in the right hand of him that sat on the throne a book written within and on the backside, sealed with seven seals. And I saw a strong angel proclaiming with a lour voice, Who is worthy to open the book, and to loose the seals thereof? And no man in heaven, nor in earth, neither under the earth, was able to open the book, neither to look thereon. And I wept much, because no man was found worthy to open and to read the book, neither to look thereon. And one of the elders saith unto me, Weep not: behold, the Lion of the tribe of Juda, the Root of David, hath prevailed to open the book, and to loose the seven seals thereof. Rev. 5:1-5.

And I saw in the right hand of him that sat on the throne, a book. The Almighty God, seated on His throne and holding a book in His right hand. The book was not a blank, but was full of writing, known only to God, the writer, and never given to any person. This book was sealed with seven seals, indicating that it contained secrets; and was kept in the right hand of God that no one might discover the secrets;

secrets kept from all the human family down to that time.

A strong angel; but he could not open the book. With a great voice, indicating great earnestness and anxiety; crying out, Who is worthy, or has the authority, wisdom, power or ability to loose the seals that God has placed upon the book; and to open the book and reveal its secrets.

And no one in heaven, or on earth, or under the earth, no angelic being, and no earthly being, and no demon could loose the seals and reveal the secrets of God.

And I wept much. Great sorrow that no one in the whole universe was able to reveal the secrets concealed in that book.

And one of the elders said, Weep not, for there is one, only one, who is both God and man, creator and created. "The Lion that is of the tribe of Judah." The creator of David hath overcome Satan, death and hell, that He might open the book and bring salvation to men.

> And I saw in the midst of the throne and of the four living creatures, and in the midst of the elders, a Lamb standing, as though it had been slain, having seven horns, and seven eyes, which are the seven Spirits of God, sent forth into all the earth. And he came, and he taketh it out of the right hand of him that sat on the throne. And when he had taken the book, the four

A BOOK WITH SEVEN SEALS 83

living creatures and the four and twenty elders fell down before the Lamb, having each one a harp, and golden bowls full of incense, which are the prayers of the saints. Rev. 5:6-8. R. V.

And I saw in the midst of the throne: The center; that is, where God sat; and who could be there but God? And of the four living creatures: The center of their sphere of activity. And in the midst of the elders: In this central place with God, I saw a Lamb standing: Not seated on the throne. As though it had been slain: Showing evidences of having been killed, but now alive again. This is the Lamb of God, Jesus Christ, our Lord. Having seven horns: Horns indicate power; and seven indicates fullness; having all power. "All power is given unto me in heaven and in earth." Matt. 28:18. And seven eyes, which are the seven Spirits of God: To see and to do what God sees and does throughout all the earth. And he came and he taketh it: The Lamb, the Lord Jesus Christ took the book out of the hand of His Father, being "One with the Father." John 17:22. And when He had taken the book, the four living creatures and the four and twenty elders fell down before the Lamb: This would have been sacrilege, blasphemy, treason, if the Lamb was not God, One with the Father. Having each one a harp and golden bowls: A harp to make music and golden bowls full of incense, prayers of the saints; pouring out true worship before the Lamb.

> And they sing a new song, saying, Worthy art thou to take the book, and to open the seals thereof: for thou wast slain, and didst purchase unto God with thy blood men of every tribe, and tongue, and people, and nation, and madest them to be unto our God a kingdom and priests; and they reign upon the earth. Rev. 5:9-10. R. V.

And they sing a new song, saying: None of the saints except the first-fruits can sing the New Song. These singers are the saints whom our Lord raised from the dead when He arose. See Matt. 27:50-53.

Saying, worthy art thou to take the book: None else could. No human being, no angel. Christ alone could take the book and open it, and reveal the secret things of God.

"For thou wast slain, and didst purchase unto God with thy blood men of every tribe, and tongue, and people, and nation." Jesus bought men of all nations and tribes and tongues by dying; a sacrifice for them, to atone for their sins. There is no salvation, but by the Blood of Christ.

"And madest them to be unto our God a kingdom and priests." Men washed and cleansed by the Blood of Jesus Christ, though they be from every nation on earth, are formed into a new Nation, a heavenly kingdom, with God as their King; and all persons thus saved are made, "A royal priesthood." I Peter, 2:9. "To offer up spiritual sacrifices unto God." I Peter 2:5.

"And they reign upon the earth." This has reference to the Millenial reign of Christ for a thousand years on the earth. The saints, the bride, the Lamb's wife will reign with Him.

> And I saw, and I heard a voice of many angels round about the throne and the living creatures and the elders; and the number of them was ten thousand times ten thousand, and thousands of thousands; saying with a great voice, Worthy is the Lamb that hath been slain to receive the power, and riches, and wisdom, and might, and honour, and glory, and blessing. Rev. 5:11-12. R. V.

"And I saw, and I heard a voice of many angels." These angels were around the throne and the living creatures, and the elders. All the first-fruits are next to the throne; and the angels form a circular company around them.

And the number of them was ten thousand times ten thousand. This is one hundred million. Then, in addition to those, there were thousands of thousands more. This innumerable multitude were angels. The company of first-fruits were an hundred and forty and four thousand. Rev. 12:1-5.

This great multitude of angels were saying with a great voice, Worthy is the Lamb that hath been slain, to receive the power, and riches, and wisdom, and might, and honour, and glory, and blessing. All the angels in heaven shout the praises of the Lord Jesus Christ because He is God, One with the Father. And John declares, I saw and I heard this worshipping by all those angels and what they said.

> And every created thing which is in the heaven, and on the earth, and under the earth, and on the sea, and all things that are in them, heard I saying, Unto him that sitteth on the throne, and unto the Lamb, be the blessing, and the honor, and the glory, and the dominion, forever and ever. And the four living creatures said, Amen. And the elders fell down and worshipped. Rev. 5:13-14. R. V.

And every created thing which is in heaven: Angels and glorified saints in heaven are not "things." The company of first-fruits first fell down and worshipped the Lamb. And all the multitudes of angels shouted the praises of the Lamb. And all other created things in heaven, and earth and sea: I understand that these created things are "the birds that fly in midheaven." (Rev. 19:17). And on the earth: all beasts and creeping things. And under the

A BOOK WITH SEVEN SEALS 87

earth: living things that dwell under the surface of the earth. And on the sea: water fowl. And all things in the sea: fishes and living creatures of every kind. Heard I say: John heard all created things saying: Unto Him that sitteth on the throne, and unto the Lamb, be the Blessing and the glory, and the dominion, forever and ever. John heard them say this. Being in the Spirit he could hear and see things that other men could not see and hear. This looks as though the animal creation, at that time, joined in the chorus of worship and praise to God and the Lamb.

And the four living creatures in heaven said, Amen to what had just been uttered by the created things. And the four and twenty elders in heaven fell down and worshiped.

Nearly all of this chapter is an exaltation of the "Slain Lamb of God," who taketh away the sin of the world. This exaltation is by the heavenly host, and the redeemed resurrected first-fruits who see things in their true light, and see Jesus Christ one with God; and apparently all created things that were not in the transgression, praised God and the Lamb.

Men still on the earth seem to have taken no part in that wonderful time of worship. The rejoicing and worship of the Lamb recorded in this chapter must not be confounded with the time when "Every knee should bow, of things in heaven and things on earth and things under the earth; and that every tongue should confess that Jesus Christ is Lord to the glory of God the Father." Phil 2:10, 11. This last Scripture, evidently refers to the judgment day. The worship of the Lamb in heaven, in which all created things, even on, and in the sea, took a part, occurred at the time the Lamb took the book to open it. So this worship of the Lamb took place before the first seal of this book was opened, and before any of the occurrences recorded took place, at the opening of each and every seal.

The book referred to could not be the book containing the plan or work of our redemption, for that book had been fully opened before John was caught up into heaven. Our Lord had been born and crucified and resurrected, and glorified; and tens of thousands had been washed and cleansed and baptized with the Holy Ghost, and many of them were in Paradise at that time. The book of "Revelation" is certainly the book referred to.

OPENING THE SEVEN SEALS

AND I saw when the Lamb opened one of the seven seals, and I heard one of the four living creatures saying as with a voice of thunder, Come. And I saw, and behold, a white horse, and he that sat thereon had a bow; and there was given unto him a crown: and he came forth conquering and to conquer. Rev. 6:1, 2, R. V.

"And I saw when the Lamb opened one of the seven seals." John has eyes and ears open, so that he may write down all that he saw and heard. And he said, I saw the seal opened, and what followed the opening of that seal.

"And I heard one of the four living creatures saying as with the voice of thunder, Come." This voice like as of thunder implies Deity. It was from the throne, although it came through one of the living creatures. "Come." This is a command to move toward or from the commander. To come or to go. The Greek word implies either. In this case it evidently means Go, as the sequel proves, for in each case a horse and his rider went forth to destroy.

This horse was white, indicating victory, often indicating purity or righteousness. Probably in this case used to deceive the people. "And he that sat thereon had a bow." Always indicating war. "And he came forth conquering, and to conquer." He went forth to conquer by use of the bow and continued the conquest from conquering to conquer others, on and on to the end. "And there was given unto him a crown." Then he had no crown prior to this time, but one was given to him by some party who had one to give. This person cannot be the Lord Jesus for we find Him in Rev. 19:12, wearing many crowns; and it cannot be Satan, for we find him in Rev. 12:3, having seven crowns. The Lord Jesus Christ is nowhere spoken of or represented as conquering by a bow. The bow is mentioned fifty-three times in the Scriptures, and fifty-one times it is man's bow with which to kill, and once, God's bow to bring war, and this person on the white horse had a bow. This bow means war and not salvation.

We find that following this white horse and his rider, there came a red horse and his rider, and he took peace from the earth, not from a nation or two, but peace from all nations. This means a world war. This war is the inevitable consequence of the mission of the first horse and his rider, who went forth to conquer the world and succeeds in doing so. See Rev. 13:7. "And power was given him over all kindreds, and tongues and nations."

This first rider, on the white horse, received

OPENING THE SEVEN SEALS

the command from the throne to Come, or Go forth in this campaign of destruction. Who is he? Read II Thes. 2:1-10, which is as follows:

Now we beseech you, brethren, touching the coming of our Lord Jesus Christ, and our gathering together unto him; to the end that ye be not quickly shaken from your mind, nor yet be troubled, either by spirit, or by word, or by epistle as from us, as that the day of the Lord is now present; let no man beguile you in any wise: for it will not be, except the falling away come first, and the man of sin be revealed, the son of perdition, he that opposeth and exalteth himself against all that is called God or that is worshiped; so that he sitteth in the temple of God, setting himself forth as God. Remember ye not, that, when I was yet with you, I told you these things? And now ye know that which restraineth, to the end that he may be revealed in his own season. For the mystery of lawlessness doth already work: only there is one that restraineth now, until he be taken out of the way. And then shall be revealed the lawless one, whom the Lord Jesus shall slay with the breath of his mouth, and bring to naught by the manifestation of his coming; even he, whose coming is according to the working of Satan with all power and signs and lying wonders, and with all deceit of unrighteousness for them that perish; because they received not the love of the truth, that they might be saved. II Thes. 2:1-10, R. V.

"Let no man beguile you in any wise," for Christ will not come until the "Man of Sin be revealed, the son of perdition, who exalteth himself against all that is called God, or that is worshipped, so that he sitteth in the temple of God, setting himself forth as God."

No Pope has ever done this, or any other person of note, since the days of Jesus on earth; but a man will arise who will actually do this, and he will be the personal Anti-Christ, the son of perdition.

"Then shall be revealed the lawless one, whom the Lord Jesus shall slay with the breath of His mouth (not with a bow), and bring to naught by the manifestation of His coming."

This Anti-Christ has not come yet, but will be on earth and actively at work before Christ comes. This same "Man of Sin," and "Son of Perdition" is the "Little horn" in Daniel's prophesy or vision. See Dan. 7:20-22. "Even that horn that had eyes, and a mouth, that spake very great things, whose look was more stout than his fellows." [This is a person, the Anti-Christ.] "I beheld, and the same horn made war with the saints, and prevailed against them; until the Ancient of days came, and judgment was given to the saints of the Most High; and

OPENING THE SEVEN SEALS   93

the time came that the saints possessed the kingdom."

"He shall speak words against the most High, and shall wear out the saints of the most High, and think to change times and laws; and they [the saints] shall be given into his hand until a time and times and the dividing of time. [Just three years and a half.] "But the judgment shall sit, and they shall take away his dominion, to consume and destroy unto the end." Dan. 7: 25-26.

Daniel desired to know when these things should take place, and was told to "Go thy way Daniel, for the words are closed up and sealed till the time of the end." Dan. 12:4.

So we see that this person, and his work, belongs to the time of the end, or the coming of Christ, "to destroy them that destroy the earth," Rev. 11:18, and then reign Lord of all for a thousand years. Here is the Anti-Christ, who will be revealed in his time, but God now withholds until the time appointed; and then shall that wicked one be revealed. The time of this withholding will end when the first seal is broken, and the command given, "Go forth, conquering and to conquer by war, famine, and pestilence over a fourth part of the earth." Rev. 6:1-8.

All historians know that such a war has never taken place since John penned these words; but it will take place as sure as God had revealed it to John.

In Rev. 13:2, R. V., we find where and how this first rider on the white horse will get his power and crown. "The dragon gave him his power and his throne, and great authority." In Rev. 12:9, "And the great dragon was cast down, the old serpent, he that is called the Devil and Satan, the deceiver of the whole world."

We find that the Devil who has seven crowns, gave one of his crowns to the beast, or Anti-Christ, or man of sin, and also his throne, and great authority. The white horse may indicate that the rider claimed to be God and demanded worship.

War

"And when he opened the second seal, I heard the second living creature saying, Come. And another horse came forth, a red horse: and to him that sat thereon it was given to take peace from the earth, and that they should slay one another; and there was given unto him a great sword." Rev. 6:3-4, R. V.

"And when he opened the second seal I heard the second living creature saying, Come." A command from the throne to go forth, and immediately a red horse and his rider with a great sword went forth.

And to him that sat thereon it was given to take peace from the whole earth. Satan could not give this authority. None but God could give such power, or authority.

"And that they should slay one another; and

OPENING THE SEVEN SEALS 95

there was given unto him a great sword." No peace on earth anywhere. The great sword indicates terrible slaughter.

Famine

And when he opened the third seal, I heard the third living creature saying, Come. And I saw, and behold, a black horse; and he that sat thereon had a balance in his hand. And I heard as it were a voice in the midst of the four living creatures saying, a measure of wheat for a penny, and three measures of barley for a penny; and the oil and the wine hurt thou not. Rev. 6:5, 6, R. V.

"And when he had opened the third seal, I heard the third living creature saying, Come [or Go], and I saw and behold a black horse. And he that sat thereon had a balance in his hand." Indicating scarcity of food, a famine; food being sold at famine prices. A famine over one-fourth part of the earth.

"And I heard as it were a voice in the midst of the four living creatures saying." This indicates the throne declaring the high price and scarcity of food. When there is a world war, famine must follow everywhere.

Pestilence

And when he opened the fourth seal, I heard the voice of the fourth living creature saying, Come. And I saw, and behold, a pale horse: and he that sat upon him, his name was Death; and Hades followed with him. And there was given unto them authority over the fourth part of the earth, to kill with sword, and with famine, and with death, and by the wild beasts of the earth. Rev. 6:7, 8, R. V.

"And when he opened the fourth seal, the fourth living creature said, Come. And a pale horse," with death himself seated upon it, and hell followed with him. This is pestilence and all the attending sorrows, pillage, incendiary and murder that will follow in the wake of a world war, and world famine, when all laws and courts and governments are breaking down. "Death and Hell," expressive of death filling hell with victims. What three words could better express the conditions that will then exist. And there was given unto them: the riders upon the four horses, who were all working in unison, under the conqueror who rode on the white horse, and who was commanded to go forth to destroy with sword and famine and pestilence. The fullness of the Gentiles having come. The world having as fully rejected Jesus Christ as the Jews did when they killed Him; and now they are given over to the Devil and the Anti-Christ.

"Authority over the fourth part of the earth, to kill with the sword and with famine, and with death, and by the wild beasts of the earth." This kind of authority, or power is not inherent

OPENING THE SEVEN SEALS 97

in Satan or the Anti-Christ, or those four riders, but the Almighty gave the conqueror and his assistants this authority, who speedily do their work.

No human being can grasp the enormity of this tragedy. Jesus Christ reveals this awful destruction of life that is coming. Those four riders on the four horses do not represent four separate epochs, or different times in history, but are four different agencies clustered together, and at work over one-fourth part of the earth, to destroy men, women and children.

THIS EUROPEAN WAR

THE first, second and third seals have been opened, and this world war has been in full swing for three years. Peace has been taken from the earth. All nations that are not actually in the war, are talking war; and preparing for it.

The war is to spread over the fourth part of the earth. All Europe is only a third part of this territory. The actual killing with the sword, and killing with hunger, and killing with pestilence and plagues, and killing by wild beasts will spread over one-fourth part of the earth. The world famine is on, and none can stop it until it has done its work. As the war spreads, and spread it will; and the famine tightens, and tighten it will; and dead and dying will be on every side, pestilence and plagues will break out. And the wild beasts will be driven by hunger to go forth to kill and devour wherever they go. The cry of "Peace, Peace" will avail nothing. The Lord Jesus who has been trying for nineteen hundred years to win men from sin and selfishness, declared when he was here on Earth, concerning the very day in which we live, that, "When they say peace, peace, then sudden destruction cometh upon them as travail on a woman with child, and they shall not escape."

The storm has broken upon this old world because of sin, and we shall surely reap what we have sown. The sword and famine is actively killing over a part of Europe. It is dreadful beyond description. They are in great tribulation, and want peace, but peace has actually departed from the earth. There will be tremendous outcries for peace, but there will be no peace. There will be but one outcome of this present phase of the war, and that will come according to the word of the Lord. No other way. Watch and you will see.

We will continue to study this wonderful Book of Revelation which will tell us all we can know of conditions until the final working out of the problem. Many parts now rioting in pleasure, money making and selfishness, will soon know the sorrows that France, Belgium, Servia, Roumania and Russia know. The whole world is now in the condition that Jerusalem and Judea was in the last days of Jeremiah's prophecy. They had defied God and their sins were so great and numerous that God would not hear their prayers, and they had to go to Babylon and die there; and their country was destroyed.

Knowing the scriptures concerning our day, the close of the "Time of the Gentiles," and believing that the Book of Revelation is a revelation and not a conundrum, we have constantly declared that Christ will not come until peace is taken from the earth, because of a world war such as we now have.

As soon as war was declared by Germany, Russia, France and Great Britain, we announced to the world that the first and second seals were opened; and that the war was on that would culminate in the forming of the Anti-Christ kingdom; and that when the third seal should be opened, famine would follow the war; and that on the opening of the fourth seal, pestilence would follow them.

Knowing that the Scriptures cannot be broken, and being pressed in the spirit, we believe of God, we wrote the article on pages 11 to 26, entitled, "The meaning and outcome of this European war," and mailed a copy of the article, and a typewritten note, to each of the Rulers of Europe, the President of the United States of America, and the Secretary of State, on the 30th day of September, 1914.

The King of Great Britain, and Secretary of State of the United States of America, wrote us a note of acknowledgment. The first week in October, 1914, we mailed a copy of the same article to each and every other Ruler on earth that we know of. We also mailed a copy to each of the large daily papers throughout the United States and Canada, and to some of the religious papers, and sent out thousands of copies among the people. We believe God directed us in all of this.

THE ANTI-CHRIST

THE next thing we see on the program is the revealing of the man of sin, or the Anti-Christ.

Now we beseech you, brethren, by the coming of our Lord Jesus Christ, and by our gathering together unto Him, that ye be not soon shaken in mind or be troubled, neither by Spirit nor by word, nor by letter as from us, as that the day of Christ is at hand. Let no man deceive you by any means: for that day shall not come except there come a falling away first, and that man of sin be revealed, the son of perdition, who opposeth and exalteth himself above all that is called God, or that is worshipped; so that he as God sitteth in the temple of God, showing himself that he is God. II Thes. 2:1-4.

The great "Falling away" refers to true holiness of heart and life in the church. No argument is necessary to convince one that true piety and devotion to Christ is almost a thing of the past. We have a form of Godliness but deny the power thereof, as the Jews had when they crucified their Saviour. The churches, as well as the outside world, are in a wild race after money and pleasure. "Lovers of pleasure more than lovers of God."

Christ is nominally accepted, but in reality rejected. Ichabod is written on the door of nearly every church in the world. Woe unto the Shepherds. The man of sin is already in the world. He went forth when the first seal was opened, before the war began. He is a Jew, of the tribe of Judah, and the Jews will accept him as the true Messiah when he comes to the throne. They will not accept any one that is not of the tribe of Judah. Jesus said to the Jews, "I am come in my Father's name and ye receive me not: if another shall come in his own name, him ye will receive." John 5:43. This refers to the Anti-Christ.

He will be a mighty man of letters, science and war. A demon possessed man having power from Satan to do signs and wonders, sufficient to convince the world that he is not a man, but God Himself. The whole world will worship him. They will not worship the true God, but they will worship the false, because he will encourage them to yield to all their passions and sin to the full. This man of sin is now known where he lives as a wonderful man, but neither he, nor the people, know his destiny yet. He will be a vile man, and shall obtain the kingdom by flatteries, and "with the arms of a flood shall they be overthrown from before him and shall be broken, yea, also the prince of the covenant.

THE ANTI-CHRIST

And after the league with him he shall work deceitfully, for he shall come up, and shall become strong with a small people, etc." Dan. 11:21, 22, 23.

In all of this, "The wicked shall do wickedly; and none of the wicked shall understand; but the wise shall understand." Dan. 12:10. The Anti-Christ will be recognized by the true children of God, before Christ comes. When the pestilence and plagues break out, you will have a fuller proof that this war is the Anti-Christ war, and that all other prophesied phenomena will follow in proper time and order.

There will be a cessation of the tribulation of those days, just before the coming of Jesus Christ. "Immediately after the tribulation of those days shall the sun be darkened and the moon shall not give her light, and the stars shall fall from heaven, and the powers of the heavens shall be shaken." [Earthquake.] Matt. 24:29.

As the temporary cessation of war, famine and pestilence comes, there will be great rejoicing over the whole world. "Peace, peace," will be on every lip. The nations will be already planning to grasp every commercial advantage, when suddenly, the earth will reel and rock and tremble, until mountains and islands have been moved from their places and destruction shall be on every nation, city and village under the sun; "And they shall not escape." The

"Sudden destruction" that will come, as travail upon a woman with child; and they shall not escape, will be this world earthquake. I Thess. 5:3.

We are now close to the Revealing of the Anti-Christ. He must be revealed to the saints before Christ comes. The great tribulation in which the saints will be overcome by the Anti-Christ, begins with this earthquake and it closes with the "Supper of the great God." Rev. 19:17.

OPENING OF THE FIFTH SEAL

AND when he had opened the fifth seal, I saw under the altar the souls of them that were slain for the word of God, and for the testimony which they held: And they cried with a loud voice, saying, How long, O Lord, holy and true, dost thou not judge and avenge our blood on them that dwell on the earth? And white robes were given unto every one of them; and it was said unto them, that they should rest yet for a little season, until their fellowservants also and their brethren, that should be killed as they were, should be fulfilled. Rev. 6:9-11.

This is a scene that takes place in heaven before the coming of Christ, and so, before the resurrection. John saw the souls of the martyred saints underneath the altar in heaven. "And they cried with a great voice saying, How long, O Lord, holy and true, dost thou not judge and avenge our blood on them that dwell on the earth?" Here are thinking, intelligent, human spirits whose bodies are still in their graves on the earth, who know something of the conditions that then exist on earth; and cry out vehemently to Christ, their master, for judgment to be meted out.

Observe that souls are seen under the altar. The soul is the thinking, intelligent, accountable man: not the body. Those had been slain, separated from their bodies. The souls are seen under the altar. They are thinking; and now enquiring of God in reference to the time when sinners are to be punished; and saints are to be rewarded; and reign on this earth for a thousand years. "How long, O Lord", Here they are enquiring as to time. Is the time not about expired? How long are we still to wait? And the answer comes; "Only a little season," until the last saint that shall ever be put to death for his integrity to God and the Lamb, shall be accomplished. And then the Kingdom shall be given to the saints.

White Robes

And a white robe was given to each of them, preparatory to their descent to the earth with Christ at His coming, to raise and glorify their bodies. "But I would not have you to be ignorant, brethren, concerning them which are asleep, that ye sorrow not, even as others which have no hope. For if we believe that Jesus died and rose again, even so them also which sleep in Jesus will God bring with Him." I Thes. 4:13-14.

OPENING OF THE FIFTH SEAL

We must keep in mind the conditions of the earth at this time, in connection with this heavenly scene. The world war is raging, and famine and pestilence destroying the people, and rebellion against God is rampant. This outcry from the unresurrected saints in heaven, while their bodies are still on the earth, has a peculiar significance. How long is this work of Satan and wicked men to continue. Is it not high time for God to stop all this slaughter and punish men for their wickedness? The horrible conditions on earth seem to be known by the saints in heaven, and causes this outcry. And those souls were robed in white. This robing of the saints in heaven at this juncture is very significant. It comes just before the resurrection of their bodies, and preparatory to their descent to the earth with Christ to be clothed upon with the new heavenly body, like unto Christ's glorious body. I Cor. 15:44, 48, 49. These are the words of God concerning the souls in heaven, and the bodies on earth. Robing the souls in heaven takes place under the opening of the fifth seal; and the resurrection takes place under the opening of the sixth seal. The saints on earth will know nothing of the opening of the fifth seal, or this heavenly scene, where the souls are all robed and ready for their descent to the earth, with their Lord.

Those souls seen under the altar when the fifth seal is opened, proves that the first resurrection has not taken place yet; after the five seals have been opened. And those souls under the altar, could not be the persons beheaded because they would not worship the beast, neither his image, neither had received his mark upon their foreheads, or in their hands: because at this time the Anti-Christ and his kingdom has not appeared; and no person has yet received his mark, nor has been asked to worship him, under pain of death.

The beast kingdom does not appear until all the seals have been opened; and until all the seven trumpets have been sounded. See Rev. 11:15, and Rev. 13:16, 17.

The resurrected persons found in heaven out of every kindred, and tongue, and people, and nation, Rev. 5:9, 10, before the first seal was opened, are the first-fruits, who came out of their graves at the time Jesus arose from the dead. The first resurrection will take place when the sixth seal is opened.

The beheaded saints are resurrected, and appear on the sea of glass before the throne, having the harps of God; and singing the praises of God and the Lamb. Rev. 15:2-4. This is after the beast has finished marking his own; and has killed the saints.

The earthquake and the three signs which will notify the saints of His coming, are the next things on the program.

OPENING OF THE SIXTH SEAL

AND I beheld when he had opened the sixth seal, and, lo, there was a great earthquake; and the sun became black as sackcloth of hair, and the moon became as blood; And the stars of heaven fell unto the earth, even as a fig tree casteth her untimely figs, when she is shaken of a mighty wind. And the heaven departed as a scroll when it is rolled together; and every mountain and island were moved out of their places. And the kings of the earth, and the great men, and the rich men, and the chief captains, and the mighty men, and every bondman, and every free man, hid themselves in the dens and in the rocks of the mountains; And said to the mountains and rocks, Fall on us and hide us from the face of him that sitteth on the throne, and from the wrath of the Lamb: For the great day of his wrath is come; and who shall be able to stand? Rev. 6:12-17.

The earthquake will come like a thunderbolt from a clear sky. As it was in the days of Noah; and as it was in the days of Sodom, the people were busy in all earthly pursuits of self and sin, and knew not until the flood came on the antedeluvians; and the fire fell on Sodom; so the world will not know until the earthquake comes, and the earth reels as a drunken man. Isa. 24:20. This world will be in a mad rush to conclude the war; each nation in their own way; to trample down their foes and build themselves upon the ruins. But suddenly the crash will come to every city, town and village; and the armies and navies throughout the whole world. Buildings will go to pieces like eggshells. Bridges will be smashed to pieces. Railroads torn up and covered with debris. Telegraph lines and cables torn to pieces. Mountains and islands moved out of their places. Trains all over the world ditched and destroyed, and tempestuous storms at sea; the sea and waves roaring. Fire will break out in all cities, and their smoke shall go up as pillars toward heaven.

"And I will show wonders in the heavens and in the earth, blood and fire, and pillars of smoke. The sun shall be turned into darkness and the moon into blood before the great and terrible day of the Lord come." Joel 2:30, 31. The dead and dying will be on every side, while the earth rocks and reels. God shaking terribly the earth. "And they shall go into the holes of the rocks, and into the caves of the earth for fear of the Lord, and for the glory

OPENING OF THE SIXTH SEAL 111

of His majesty, when He ariseth to shake terribly the earth." Isa. 2:19.

Black as Sackcloth

The world will be enshrouded in darkness, the sun having become black as sackcloth of hair, and the moon become as a blood spot, and the stars falling to the earth. O! what a time that will be. Such a condition as never was known on all the earth before. "But the word of the Lord standeth sure." "The scriptures cannot be broken." "My word shall not pass away."

God's children will pass through this scene. Jesus Christ speaking of it says, "Watch ye therefore and pray always that ye may be accounted worthy to escape all these things that shall come to pass, and to stand before the Son of Man." Luke 21:36. They are also commanded to lift up their heads for their redemption (resurrection and translation) draweth nigh.

This earthquake and signs, when they come, will be proof that the sixth seal is opened. Out of this awful earth confusion and destruction, and the war, famine, pestilence and wild beasts let loose, the first resurrection will take place, and the living saints will be translated. We think the world will know nothing of the translation, or anything of the resurrection, but will suppose the missing ones have been buried in the ruins somewhere. The wicked knew nothing of our Lord's resurrection, and they probably will know nothing of the first resurrection. There was an earthquake before our Lord's resurrection, and there will be this earthquake before our resurrection. So the saints will certainly "Come up out of great tribulation." The foolish virgins will have to go through this great tribulation because they were not ready for translation, at His Coming.

The signs of His coming given by our Lord in Mathew, Mark and Luke, follow this earthquake, and indicate that He is at the door.

The saints are gone from the earth, the spirit, soul and body of every one of them who had lived upon this earth from Adam down to that same day in which Jesus came and defeated death and the Devil, and took His own to be where He was, "forever with the Lord," with the exception of the two mentioned in Rev. 11:3, "my two witnesses" whom we will consider later in the order in which they are introduced.

We call your attention to this fact that only two saints are now left upon the earth. God's people are the salt of the earth; and the light of the world. But this salt and light is now gone. The two angels who destroyed Sodom and Gomorrah took Lot and his wife and two daughters out of Sodom and sent them to Zoar, saying, "Haste thee, escape thither; for I cannot do anything till thou come thither." Gen. 19:22. God could not destroy Noah and his family with the wicked, and so he had him build the Ark; but immediately after they were safely shut in the Ark, and God had closed the door of the Ark, the flood came and destroyed all outside. Now that but two righteous men are left upon this earth, What next?

SEALING THE 144,000

AND after these things I saw four angels standing on the four corners of the earth, holding the four winds of the earth, that the wind should not blow on the earth, nor on the sea, nor on any tree. And I saw another angel ascending from the east, having the seal of the living God: and he cried with a loud voice to the four angels to whom it was given to hurt the earth and the sea, Saying, Hurt not the earth, neither the sea, nor the trees, till we have sealed the servants of our God in their foreheads. And I heard the number of them which were sealed: and there were sealed a hundred and forty and four thousand of all the tribes of the children of Israel. Of the tribe of Judah were sealed twelve thousand. Of the tribe of Reuben were sealed twelve thousand. Of the tribe of Gad were sealed twelve thousand. Of the tribe of Aser were sealed twelve thousand. Of the tribe of Nepthalim were sealed twelve thousand. Of the tribe of Manasseh were sealed twelve thousand. Of the tribe of Simeon were

SEALING THE 144,000

sealed twelve thousand. Of the tribe of Levi were sealed twelve thousand. Of the tribe of Issachar were sealed twelve thousand. Of the tribe of Zebulun were sealed twelve thousand. Of the tribe of Joseph were sealed twelve thousand. Of the tribe of Benjamin were sealed twelve thousand. Rev. 7:1-8.

Here are four angels, one in each of the four quarters of the earth, with authority to hurt the earth and the sea. They were already holding the wind so it could not blow on the earth or the sea or on any tree. God only knows what would happen to this earth if there was no more wind. Probably everything would become stagnant, and death would ensue.

A fifth angel appears and calls a halt, until he should seal 144,000 men in their foreheads. These men are called the "Servants of God." If they were the Lord's, they would have been translated, for all who are the Lord's, are to be, "changed in a moment, in the twinkling of an eye, at the last trump." I Cor. 15-52; The trump that closes the time of the Gentiles.

God calls the King of Babylon "My servant," when He sent the Babylonian army to take Jerusalem. Jer. 25:9; Jer. 27:6; and Jer. 4:10. God calls Israel "My servant," continually, because He had chosen Abraham and his seed for a purpose, and He also calls them a stubborn and rebellious people. They were servants but not saints. The 144,000 are all Abraham's seed, and so are His servants, to now do His will on Earth. Twelve thousand from each of the twelve tribes, and He has sealed them for a purpose, at the close of the "Times of the Gentiles."

Those chosen ones are to be grafted into the true olive tree at the proper time. They are now selected as a bunch of grafts and marked. We will watch for them as we study this revelation of Jesus Christ. They remain on earth to re-populate the earth with Israelites, when the rest are destroyed. "For He will destroy all them that know not God." Rev. 11:18.

The Translation

> After this I beheld, and, lo, a great multitude which no man could number, of all nations, and kindreds, and people, and tongues, stood before the throne, and before the Lamb, clothed with white robes and palms in their hands; And cried with a loud voice, saying, Salvation to our God which sitteth upon the throne, and unto the Lamb. And all the angels stood round about the throne, and about the elders and the four beasts, and fell before the throne on their

SEALING THE 144,000

faces, and worshipped God, Saying, Amen: Blessing, and glory, and wisdom, and thanksgiving, and honour, and power and might, be unto our God forever and ever. Amen. And one of the elders answered, saying unto me, What are these which are arrayed in white robes? and whence came they? And I said unto him, Sir, thou knowest. And he said to me, These are they which came out of great tribulation, and have washed their robes, and made them white in the blood of the Lamb. Therefore are they before the throne of God, and serve Him day and night in His temple: and He that sitteth on the throne shall dwell among them. They shall hunger no more, neither thirst any more; neither shall the sun light on them, nor any heat. For the Lamb which is in the midst of the throne shall feed them, and shall lead them unto living fountains of waters, and God shall wipe all tears from their eyes. Rev. 7:9-17.

John watched the sealing of the 144,000 and heard the number of them, and then, behold, a great multitude which no man could number, from all nations, and kindreds, and people and tongues, stood before the throne, and before the Lamb.

While the angel was sealing the 144,000 Israelites, the Lord Jesus had raised the dead, and translated the living saints and took them straight to the throne of God, and presented them to His Father. And here we see them rejoicing and praising God. This is the first resurrection. The saints are not waiting or wandering in the air, but are with God in heaven; and all the angels are present, and take part in the Jubilee. And Jubilee it is, for they are loosed from all sin, and bondage, and death and the devil, from all earthly conditions, forevermore. Free! Free! Free! Forever with the Lord.

"Therefore are they before the throne of God, and serve Him day and night in His Temple: and He that sitteth on the throne shall dwell among them. * * * And the Lamb which is in the midst of the throne shall feed them, and shall lead them unto living fountains of waters, and God shall wipe away all tears from their eyes."

OPENING OF THE SEVENTH SEAL

AND when he opened the seventh seal, there followed a silence in heaven about the space of half an hour. And I saw the seven angels that stand before God; and there were given unto them seven trumpets. And another angel came and stood *over the altar,* having a golden censer; and there was given unto him much incense that he should add it unto the prayers of all the saints upon the golden altar which was before the throne. And the smoke of the incense, with the prayers of the saints, went up before God out of the angel's hand. And the angel taketh the censer; and he filled it with the fire of the altar, and cast it upon the earth; and there followed thunders and voices, and lightnings and an earthquake. Rev. 8:1-5, R. V.

"There was silence in heaven for half an hour,"—All the saints around the throne, and all the angels with them in the Jubilee scene, are hushed into silence for about half an hour. Then seven angels that stand before God in heaven were given seven trumpets. Then another angel came and stood at God's altar in heaven, he having a golden censer, and there was given unto him much incense, that he should offer the incense with the prayers of all saints upon the golden altar which was before the throne. *This is a prayer meeting of all of the assembled resurrected saints before the throne of God in heaven, from every nation, kindred, people and tongue.* After the silence for half an hour, what a volume of prayer ascended to God. "And the smoke of the incense, with the prayers of the saints, ascended up before God out of the angel's hand." *This is the purest of worship before the Almighty.* What a prayer meeting that will be, when all the saints arrive at home, and stand or kneel before their God, and his throne, surrounded by all the angels of heaven, *and worship God.*

Then the angel took the censer and filled it with fire from off God's altar and cast it into the earth, where Satan and his followers then had full control. There were voices, and thunderings, and lightnings, and as the fire *struck the earth, there was an earthquake. Another earthquake!* This is the opening of God's battle against a world of people who will not accept God's salvation. And as the rain came down and drowned the people of Noah's day, now God sends fire in the days of the Anti-Christ.

THE SEVEN TRUMPETS

AND the seven angels that had the seven trumpets prepared themselves to sound. And the first sounded, and there followed hail and fire, mingled with blood, and they were cast upon the earth: and the third part of the earth was burnt up, and the third part of the trees was burnt up, and all green grass was burnt up. Rev. 8:6-7, R. V.

This hail and fire mingled with blood, was cast upon the earth; and it produced a *world fire* that consumed all growing crops, and one-third part of the trees, and the third part of the cities, towns and villages and country homes. This would result in a terrible *world-wide famine*. All of these judgments are world-wide.

And the second angel sounded, and as it were a great mountain burning with fire was cast into the sea; and the third part of the sea became blood; and the third part of the creatures which were in the sea and had life, died; and the third part of the ships were destroyed. Rev. 8:8-9.

Fire again, like a mountain on fire, strikes

the sea, turning the third part of the sea into blood, and brings death to all life in the third part of the sea, and destroys all the shipping in that part of the oceans.

> And the third angel sounded and there fell a great star from heaven, burning as it were a lamp, and it fell upon the third part of the rivers, and upon the fountains of waters; and the name of the star is called wormwood; and the third part of the waters became wormwood; and many men died of the waters, because they were made bitter. Rev. 8:10-11.

Who can imagine the distress and dismay of the people when the fresh water in the rivers, creeks, ponds, lakes, reservoirs and wells, over one-third part of every nation, kindred, people, and tongue has been turned into wormwood? Here is a *series of facts,* not fiction. All these things *will come to pass,* at the time appointed.

> And the fourth angel sounded, and the third part of the sun was smitten, and the third part of the moon, and the third part of the stars; that the third part of them should be darkened, and the day should not shine for the third part of it, and the night in like manner. Rev. 8:12, R. V.

Here is another series of facts that will surely come to pass. These are things that must shortly come to pass. Four judgments have fallen on the rebellious people. Fire on land and fire on the sea. The sun, moon and stars smitten, and the fresh water turned to wormwood, bringing dearth, famine and death.

And I beheld, and heard an angel flying through the midst of heaven, saying with a loud voice, *Woe, woe, woe,* to the inhabiters of the earth by reason of the other voices of the trumpet of the three angels which are yet to sound! Rev. 8:13.

What else but *woe! woe!* can come to a people who will fight God to the last trench?

OPENED THE BOTTOMLESS PIT

AND the fifth angel sounded, and I saw a star fall from heaven unto the earth; and to him was given the key of the bottomless pit. And he opened the bottomless pit; and there arose a smoke out of the pit, as the smoke of a great furnace; and the sun and the air were darkened by reason of the smoke of the pit. And there came out of the smoke locusts upon the earth: and unto them was given power, as the scorpions of the earth have power. And it was commanded them that they should not hurt the grass of the earth, neither any green thing, neither any tree; but only those men which have not the seal of God in their foreheads. And to them it was given that they should not kill them, but that they should be tormented five months: and their torment was as the torment of a scorpion, when he striketh a man. And in those days shall men seek death, and shall not find it; and shall desire to die, and death shall flee from them. And the shapes of the locusts were like

OPENED THE BOTTOMLESS PIT 125

unto horses prepared unto battle; and on their heads were as it were crowns like gold, and their faces were as the faces of men. And they had hair as the hair of women, and their teeth were as the teeth of lions. And they had breastplates, as it were breastplates of iron; and the sound of their wings was as the sound of chariots of many horses running to battle. And they had tails like unto scorpions, and there were stings in their tails; and their power was to hurt men five months. And they had a king over them, which is the angel of the bottomless pit, whose name in the Hebrew tongue is Abaddon, but in the Greek tongue hath his name Apollyon. Rev. 9:1-11.

This bottomless pit is hell, and it is the melted lava in the heart of this earth. The star that fell to the earth was an angel sent with a key to the door of the bottomless pit; and he went straight to this earth and opened the door of the pit; and smoke came out of the pit, shutting out the sunlight from this earth because of real smoke that filled the air. And living creatures came out of the smoke upon the earth. These living creatures came with the smoke out of the bottomless pit where they lived in fire; and they had a king over them who is the angel of the bottomless pit, whose name in the Hebrew tongue is Abaddon, but in the Greek tongue, his name is Apollyon.

The door to this place is opened, and the inhabitants are let loose upon the earth by orders from heaven, sending an angel and the right key to open the door. These living creatures, or demons, are sent to torment men for five months, or, one hundred and fifty days. Their torment is so terrible that men will seek for death and cannot die; desire to die, and death shall flee from them. These demons could kill them, but God will not permit them to do so; only to torment the men who will not serve God.

The 144,000 Israelites who were sealed in their foreheads by an angel are among the men still on the earth, and the demons were commanded of God not to touch one of them. They are under the seal of the Almighty. They are not the first fruits, and they are not the Bride. They are human beings still in the body, selected, marked and preserved for a purpose. God will use them at the proper time. They are servants of God.

The description of these creatures from the pit is terrible. Their shape is like unto horses, with crowns like gold on their heads. Not gold, but like it; with faces like men, and long hair like women, and teeth like lions, with wings and tails. To chase and sting men for five months.

God, who knows that there is a *Hell*, and *Devil*, will open the door of hell, and let men know that there are demons and a hell, at that time. We believe that this opening of the bottomless pit is to convince men of the reality of demons and a literal hell. After men are chased and stung by demons, and Satan in the lead for one hundred and fifty days and nights, wanting to die, trying to kill themselves but cannot, one would think they would turn to God, repenting and confessing their sins, that they might be saved, for God wants to save them.

THE LAST WAR

NE woe is past; and, behold, there come two woes more hereafter. And the sixth angel sounded, and I heard a voice from the four horns of the golden altar which is before God, saying to the sixth angel which had the trumpet, Loose the four angels which are bound in the great river Euphrates. And the four angels were loosed, which were prepared for an hour, and a day, and a month, and a year, for to slay the third part of men. And the number of the army of the horsemen were two hundred thousand thousand: and I heard the number of them. And thus I saw the horses in the vision, and them that sat on them, having breastplates of fire, and of jacinth, and brimstone: and the heads of the horses were as the heads of lions; and out of their mouths issued fire and smoke and brimstone. By these three was the third part of men killed, by the fire, and by the smoke, and by the brimstone, which issued out of their mouths. For their power is in their mouth,

THE LAST WAR

and in their tails; for their tails were like unto serpents, and had heads, and with them they do hurt. And the rest of the men which were not killed by these plagues yet repented not of the works of their hands, that they should not worship devils, and idols of gold, and silver, and brass, and stone, and of wood: which neither can see, nor hear, nor walk; neither repented they of their murders, nor of their sorceries, nor of their fornication, nor of their thefts. Rev. 9:12-21.

"And I heard a voice from the four horns of the golden altar which is before God."

This is God commanding the sixth angel to loose, or let loose a mighty force that hitherto had been held in restraint; but had been prepared for this very year, month, and day, and hour, to go forth to slay the third part of men. This prepared force is an army of horsemen, two hundred million strong. This army was bound in a country, or countries where two hundred million men had lived and been prepared for this tremendous last, and greatest war ever known on earth. And the countries referred to were not on this side of the great river Euphrates, but beyond it.

The man on the white horse in Revelation 6:2, went out to conquer, and to conquer. Peace was taken from the earth, famine and pestilence came on. The Lord has taken the saints out of this world, and into heaven, then the judgments of God were poured out on the fighting, rebellious people remaining on the earth who have given themselves wholly to sin, without restraint. The man on the white horse must conquer the whole world. Europe, North and South America, and Africa are under his control at this time. All Asia, seeing the trend of affairs, have prepared for the conflict; and now God lets them loose. From India, Persia, China, Russia, and Japan they go forth, all united, and the third part of men are killed.

John saw this army go forth. He heard the number of them, and describes them the best he could, knowing nothing of modern warfare; but he saw smoke, fire and brimstone, and men dying. We believe the things described as men on horses, with death-dealing power in mouths and tails, will be machine guns mounted on wheels. This army will go forth at the time appointed; and it will go from Asia, and "destroy the third part of men." The rest of the men which were not killed by these plagues, including all the plagues God has sent upon them, repented not of the works of their hands, that they should not worship devils (for they will be doing this), and idols of gold, and silver and brass, and stone, and of wood. "Neither repented they of their murders, nor

THE LAST WAR

of their sorceries, nor their fornication, nor of their thefts." These are the sins of our day. They will not repent, and without repentance and turning from sin, there is no salvation.

All Asia is now awake and taking lessons from Europe how to kill men. Japan is armed and ready, and now training the Chinese. India is, as a tiger, planning. Asiatic Russia will join in with her neighbors, and by the time the United States and Europe have fastened their grip on all the rest of the world, Asia will be ready for them.

Woe, woe to this old world. God has spoken, the time has come. The closing of the sixth thousand years of man's rule on earth is being enacted, and the world knows it not. "O ye hypocrites, ye can discern the face of the sky, but can ye not discern the signs of the times?" Matt. 16:3.

THE SEVEN THUNDERS

AND I saw another strong angel coming down out of heaven, arrayed with a cloud; and the rainbow was upon his head, and his face was as the sun, and his feet as pillars of fire; and he had in his hand a little book open: and he set his right foot upon the sea, and his left foot upon the earth; and he cried with a great voice, as a lion roareth: and when he cried, the seven thunders uttered their voices. And when the seven thunders uttered their voices, I was about to write: and I heard a voice from heaven saying, Seal up the things which the seven thunders uttered, and write them not. Rev. 10:14, R. V.

This mighty angel has some of the appearances of Christ. His face as the face of the sun, and his feet as pillars of fire; and a rainbow was upon his head. He is Mighty: and he cried with a loud voice and his cry was as a lion roaring. He set his right foot on the sea, his left still on the earth, indicating that momentous things were about to fall on the earth and sea. He stands on both.

THE SEVEN THUNDERS 133

Seven thunders utter their voices; and John took his pen to write down what the seven thunders had said, and was forbidden to write them. God from heaven said unto him, "Seal up those things which the seven thunders uttered, and write them not." These seven thunders probably spoke of the awful things that would take place during the conflict between all Asia, two-thirds of the population of the world, including all Mohammedans, on the one side, against Europe, North and South America, and Africa. Those scenes are too black for contemplation. And so they are sealed up.

> And the angel which I saw standing upon the sea and upon the earth lifted up his right hand to heaven, and sware by him that liveth forever and ever, who created the heaven and the things that are therein, and the earth and the things that are therein, and the sea and the things that are therein, that there shall be time no longer: but in the days of the voice of the seventh angel, when he is about to sound, then is finished the mystery of God, according to the good tidings which he declared to his servants the prophets. Rev. 10:5-7, R. V.

Then the angel lifted his hand to heaven and swore by Him that liveth forever and ever, the maker of all things, that there should be time no longer. Man's time is up; and God's time has come. Everything now will go God's way. Men will bite the dust: God shall reign. The seventh angel is still to sound, and other terrible closing scenes will come before us; but this angel, with one foot on land and one on the sea, now declares that, "In the days of the voice of the seventh angel, when he shall begin to sound, the mystery of God is finished, as He hath declared to His servants and prophets."

Everything will be closed up according to God's prophecy. The world has not yet been fully conquered by the Anti-Christ, but the conflict is on, and Satan and his chief, the Anti-Christ, must reign supreme for a time. It will all be worked out under the sounding of the seventh angel.

THE TWO WITNESSES

AND there was given me a reed like unto a rod: and the angel stood, saying, Rise, and measure the temple of God, and the altar, and them that worship therein. But the court which is without the temple leave out, and measure it not; for it is given unto the Gentiles: and the holy city shall they tread under foot forty and two months. And I will give power unto my two witnesses, and they shall prophesy a thousand two hundred and threescore days, clothed in sackcloth. These are the two olive trees and the two candlesticks standing before the God of the earth. And if any man will hurt them, fire proceedeth out of their mouth, and devoureth their enemies: and if any man will hurt them, he must in this manner be killed. These have power to shut heaven, that it rain not in the days of their prophecy: and have power over waters to turn them to blood and to smite the earth with all plagues, as often as they will. And when they shall have finished their testimony, the beast that ascendeth out of the bottomless pit shall make war against them, and shall overcome them, and kill them. And their dead bodies shall lie in the street of the great city, which spiritually is called Sodom and Egypt, where also our Lord was crucified. And they of the people and kindreds and tongues and nations shall see their dead bodies three days and an half, and shall not suffer their dead bodies to be put in graves. And they that dwell upon the earth shall rejoice over them, and make merry, and shall send gifts one to another; because these two prophets tormented them that dwelt on the earth. And after three days and an half the Spirit of life from God entered into them, and they stood upon their feet; and great fear fell upon them which saw them. And they heard a great voice from heaven saying unto them, Come up hither. And they ascended up to heaven in a cloud; and their enemies beheld them. And the same hour was there a great earthquake, and the tenth part of the city fell, and in the earthquake were slain of men seven thousand: and the remnant were affrighted, and gave glory to the God of heaven. The second woe is past, and, behold, the third woe cometh quickly. Rev. 11:1-14.

THE TWO WITNESSES 137

"And there was given me a reed, like unto a rod, and the angel stood, saying:" Probably the same angel that stood on the sea and the earth. "Arise, and measure the temple of God, and the altar, and them that worship therein." The temple in Jerusalem, having been rebuilt, Israelites, not Gentiles, are worshipping therein, according to the Law of Moses. We believe these worshippers are the 144,000 sealed Israelites, and they are the nominal church, the only church of God on earth at this time; but they have not yet accepted Jesus Christ as the Messiah. They are the elect remnant that shall be saved.

"But the court which is without the temple leave out, and measure it not; for it is given unto the Gentiles; and the holy city shall they tread under foot forty and two months." This is not a scene taking place, or one that has taken place, but a declaration of what is to take place, and continue for forty and two *months,* not years. God is not speaking mysteriously, but plainly; just forty and two months: during the reign of the Anti-Christ.

Two Witnesses

"And I will give power unto my two witnesses." These two witnesses will be men of that day, saints of God, remaining on earth for this very time and work. As God raised up Moses, and John the Baptist, in their day, so He will raise up these two men, thoroughly fitted for this time. God is not so limited, that He must bring back Moses or Elijah. God has not brought back any saint in the past, to do some work that could not be done without them. When He wants a man, He raises up a man for that place, as He raised Abraham, Noah, David, Moses, Daniel, Jeremiah and John, Peter and Paul. None of these holy men were brought back to earth because God had not a man to fill the place. When God needs a man He prepares one for the place. Neither will Judas be brought back to be the Anti-Christ. God only, will resurrect Judas: the Devil cannot. But the Devil can find men on earth bad enough to fill the place of Anti-Christ.

The two witnesses are to be in place, and action, for a thousand, two hundred and threescore *days,* clothed in sackcloth. This is exactly forty-two months, and is the same *forty-two months* in which Jerusalem will be trodden under foot by the Gentiles. These two witnesses will be God's two candlesticks and the two olive trees of that day. All other salt, and light of the earth, having been taken out of the world, these will stand before the God of the earth. "Satan is the God of this world who hath blinded the minds of them which believe not." II Cor. 4:4. He and the Anti-Christ are to have control of this earth for three years and a half, or *forty-two months,* as we will see in another chapter; and when he is in control, he will have possession of Jerusalem, and having his throne there will pollute the whole city, except the temple and them that dwell therein. During this time, just forty-two months, the two witnesses will shine for God. They shall prophesy during the whole twelve hundred and sixty days, clothed in sackcloth. No gaiety, no dress parade, no trifling, no jesting, no foolish talking, no compromising with the devil! They will be in dead earnest resisting evil. If any man attempts to hurt them, fire will proceed out of their mouths and consume him. "And if any man will hurt them, he must in this way be killed." These two witnesses have power to shut heaven, that it rain not in the days of their prophecy." This rather implies that there will be no rain for three years and a half, or during the whole of the Anti-Christ's reign.

They have also "power over waters to turn them to blood, and to smite the earth with all plagues," as often as they will. And when they shall have finished their testimony, at the end of the forty-two months, and just at the close of the Anti-Christ's career, "The beast that ascendeth out of the bottomless pit shall make war against them, and shall overcome them, and kill them." This is the scarlet-colored beast upon which the harlot sat. Here is the first mention of *this beast* that will be in full control of Jerusalem and the world, at the time that the two witnesses are finishing their work. But as we are not considering a scene, but only stating what will take place at the time Jerusalem is trodden under foot of the Gentiles, we will study this beast fully when he appears.

Dead Bodies in the Street

"And their dead bodies shall lie in the street of the great city which is spiritually called Sodom and Egypt, where also our Lord was crucified." Jerusalem at this time will be a Sodom. The two witnesses are lying dead in the street, and the people from different nations then living there shall see their dead bodies three days and a half, and shall not permit their dead bodies to be put in graves; and news of their death having been telegraphed all over the world, all nations will "Rejoice and make merry, because these two prophets tormented them that dwell on the earth." The plagues brought by the two witnesses have been world plagues, and the world has known from whence they came. Now that the two men are dead, the world rejoices, supposing that their troubles will cease. But after three days and a half, the spirit of life from God, entered into them and they stood upon their feet, and great fear fell upon them that saw them. And they heard a voice from heaven saying unto them, "Come up hither," and they ascended up to heaven in a cloud; and their enemies beheld them. In the same hour, there was a great earthquake, in which seven thousand men were killed, and part of the city destroyed. The people were terrified, and acknowledged that God had done this. All of this will be worked out exactly as God has given it to us, and at the time appointed. Not a word shall fail.

"The second woe is past; and behold, the third woe cometh quickly." God is now working fast. No more winking at sin. Man's day is ending, and Christ shall reign for a thousand years.

CHRIST TAKES THE KINGDOM

AND the seventh angel sounded: and there were great voices in heaven, saying, the kingdoms of this world are become the kingdoms of our Lord, and of His Christ; and He shall reign forever and ever. And the four and twenty elders which sat before God on their seats, fell upon their faces and worshipped God, saying, We give Thee thanks, O Lord God Almighty, which art, and wast, and art to come; because Thou hast taken to Thee Thy great power, and hast reigned. And the nations were angry, and Thy wrath is come, and the time of the dead, that they should be judges, and that Thou shouldst give reward unto Thy servants the prophets, and to the saints, and them that fear Thy name, small and great; and shouldst destroy them which destroy the earth. And the temple of God was opened in heaven, and there was seen in His temple the ark of His testament; and there were lightnings, and voices, and thunderings, and an earthquake, and great hail. Rev. 11:15-19.

CHRIST TAKES THE KINGDOM

This is a scene in heaven. "And there were great voices in heaven, saying, The kingdoms of this world are become the kingdoms of our Lord, and of His Christ; and He shall reign forever and ever." When the heir to a throne is crowned, there is great rejoicing by his friends. There will be shouting in heaven among the saints and angels when all the kingdoms on earth become the kingdom of God, and Christ shall reign forever. No man will ever reign on earth again. "The government shall be upon His shoulders and His Name shall be called, Wonderful, Counsellor, The Mighty God, The Everlasting Father, The Prince of Peace." Isa. 9:6.

And the four and twenty elders which sat before God on their thrones fell upon their faces and worshipped God, saying, "We give Thee thanks, O Lord God Almighty, which art, and wast, and art to come; because Thou hast taken to Thee Thy great power, and hast reigned." The elders are the representatives of all the saints in heaven, and thus declare their joy that the time has at last come, when God and Christ have asserted their rights, and have taken the kingdom. They also declare that "The nations were angry, and Thy wrath is come, and the time of the dead, that they should be judged, and that Thou shouldst give reward unto thy servants the prophets, and to the saints, and them that fear Thy name, small and great." They also declare that the time has come, that God, "Should destroy them which destroy the earth." This implies that the wars, raging for years, ever since the Anti-Christ went forth to conquer, when peace was taken from the earth, shall be stopped by God destroying the men who have been, and are destroying the earth. This is the work to be done; not a reformation, not a sweeping revival. God's wrath is come. It was mercy, patience, long-suffering, pleading with sinners, "Why will ye die?" Now it is wrath with the men who will not repent, will not hearken, will not hear God. "And there were lightnings, and voices, and thunderings, and an earthquake, and great hail." The earth trembles greatly as the *wrath* of God kindles. From this time on, God and the Lamb will have their way on this earth, closing man's rule, or misrule, forever.

THE WOMAN CLOTHED WITH THE SUN

AND there appeared a great wonder in heaven; a woman clothed with the sun, and the moon under her feet, and upon her head a crown of twelve stars: And she being with child cried, travailing in birth, and pained to be delivered. And there appeared another wonder in heaven; and behold a great red dragon, having seven heads and ten horns, and seven crowns upon his heads. And his tail drew the third part of the stars of heaven, and did cast them to the earth and the dragon stood before the woman which was ready to be delivered, for to devour her child as soon as it was born. And she brought forth a man child, who was to rule all nations with a rod of iron: and her child was caught up unto God and to His throne. Rev. 12:1-5.

This woman represents the Church of God in all ages, from Adam down to the last man that will be washed in the Blood of Christ.

The crown of twelve stars on her head, indicates that she is of the twelve tribes of Israel;

and also is of the twelve apostles of the Lamb. And this is clearly proven by Rev. 21:9-12, "And there came unto me one of the seven angels which had the seven vials full of the seven last plagues, and talked with me, saying, Come hither, and I will show thee the bride the Lamb's wife. And he carried me away in the spirit to a great and high mountain, and he showed me that great city, the holy Jerusalem, descending out of heaven from God: and her light was like unto a stone most precious, even like a jasper stone, clear as crystal; and had a wall great and high, and had twelve gates, and at the gates twelve angels, and names written thereon, which are the names of the *twelve tribes of the children of Israel.*"

This is the Bride

This is the bride, the Lamb's wife, including the saved people from all of the twelve tribes of Israel.

"And the wall of the city had *twelve foundations,* and in them the names of the *twelve apostles of the Lamb.* Rev. 21:14.

This city is the bride, the Lamb's wife; and includes the *twelve apostles,* who are foundations of the true Church of God: and the twelve gates of the city are the *twelve tribes of Israel,* or indicate that the twelve tribes of Israel are there.

The Holy Spirit declares through the Apostle

Paul, to the saints at Ephesus, "Now therefore ye are no more strangers and foreigners, but fellow-citizens with the saints, and of the household of God; and are built upon the foundation of the *apostles, and prophets,* Jesus Christ Himself being the *chief cornerstone."* Eph. 2:19-20.

Here is positive proof that the Gentile believers are builded upon the same foundation; and this foundation is not the apostles only, but the prophets also. And these are the foundation stones of the *only true Church of God: the bride the Lamb's wife,* the holy Jerusalem. And the woman with the moon under her feet, and clothed with the sun, is the *bride, the Lamb's wife.*

At this particular time when the woman appeared, with the moon under her feet; and clothed with the sun: all on earth who "Are the Lord's" have been resurrected; and all who were still in the body, and were ready for heaven, have been changed "In a moment, in the twinkling of an eye, at the last trump, (excepting the two witnesses): for the trump shall sound; and the dead shall be raised incorruptible, and we shall be changed." I Cor. 15:52. All of these are in the resurrection state, having their spiritual, heavenly bodies; and are in heaven before the throne, to be forever with the Lord. Rev. 7:9-17.

Those resurrected and glorified saints, together with the first-fruits, constitute the *Church in heaven*. This Church has the moon under her feet, and is clothed with the sun. Jerusalem which is above is free, which is the mother of us all. Gal. 4:26.

The Woman Represents the Church

The woman in Rev. 12:1, represents the Church of Jesus Christ on earth and in heaven. The saints who were in the body when their Lord came, were the Church on earth of that day. They had been actively at work on earth, for the salvation of souls, until they were changed and caught up to meet the Lord in the air. The effect of their teaching; and the good seed sown beside all waters, remained with the unsaved on earth. Many persons were under conviction for sinning, but had not yielded themselves to God. Many foolish virgins, backslidden preachers and people, were left on earth, who knew the truth. Both of these classes of persons are coming to the birth; but are not yet born of God.

A mother being with child, and dying, the child dies also. But in this case, the mother is not dead, but in heaven, with the resurrected body. See Rev. 7:9-17 and 8:1-4. Here we see the church in heaven, the living mother, praying. There was great rejoicing when they first reached the throne; later there was a great silence for half an hour; and then this great church prayer meeting, when the incense and the prayers of the saints went up to God. And what were they praying about, or for? Was it not for the children begotten, but not yet born, and on earth? The mother is here seen "Travailing in birth, and pained to be delivered. Rev. 12:2. The delivery would be on earth, as the children were born of the Spirit.

THE MAN CHILD.

THE church having been resurrected, and in heaven; and the great red dragon (the Devil) having been cast down to the earth, stands ready to devour the children as soon as they are born of God; and they have no mother on earth to care for them. All of those persons thus truly born of God, after the saints that were on earth when Jesus came, are gone; and all backslidden persons, who have wept their way back to God, "Until Christ be formed in them," anew, compose the Man-Child company. The soul is born, created anew, raised to a new life at conversion; and the body is born into the heavenly state at, or in the resurrection. This Man-Child could not be caught up to heaven without being born of God, soul and body. Dead people cannot go into heaven. "Ye must be born again." John 3:7.

The Two Witnesses

The two witnesses have been on earth since the Lord came and raised the dead and translated the living saints; and they have not been idle. They are the Peter and Paul of that time. How can the people hear without a

THE MAN CHILD   151

preacher; and how can they preach unless they be sent of God? These witnesses are immune to all plagues; and the wars then raging. They are super-men in the fullest sense of the word. They cannot be killed, for God keeps them. Fire proceeds from their mouths, and kills any man that would hurt them. They are the only persons who can go about witnessing for Jesus; and exhorting men to repent, and believe on the Lord Jesus Christ; in that day. Other men who will not take the mark, and worship the beast, are put to death. They are being searched for everywhere, to kill them. "Blessed are the dead who die in the Lord from henceforth." Rev. 14:13. The conditions, and persecution will be so terrible, that to die in the Lord will be blessed.

Miraculous Power

These two witnesses will have power to turn water into blood, and to smite the earth with plagues as often as they will. And will probably be carried about by the Spirit, as Philip was, from place to place as God wills. Angels also, will be preaching at this time; and warning men not to take the mark of the beast. See Rev. 14:9-11. Men will be exhorted not to fear men, but to fear God; and make peace with Him, by repentance, and faith in the Lord Jesus Christ. And men will fall down before God; and cry out for salvation from sin, with the full knowledge that they will be put to death by the followers of the Anti-Christ, as soon as they are discovered. And they will not try to hide themselves to prolong life: knowing that to deny Christ, to save their own lives, would cause them to lose their souls and bodies in hell.

Those will be awful days. But "Whosoever will save his life shall lose it: and whosoever will lose his life for my sake shall find it." Matt. 16:25. Men will then decide whether they will remain in sin with demons; and go to hell; or turn to God and Christ; and die as martyrs, and be forever with the Lord. "Whosoever therefore shall be ashamed of me and my words in this adulterous and sinful generation, of him also shall the Son of Man be ashamed when He cometh in the glory of His Father with the holy angels." Mark 8:38.

Multitudes will come to Christ, because of the words of the two witnesses; and of the angels; and the awful conditions that then exist. Here is the birth of the "Man-Child." Born of God, with the Devil and death standing before them. They willingly die to save their souls. And as the two witnesses later on, when slain, their bodies lie unburied in the street until God raises them to life again: so, probably the members of the Man-Child company will lie dead until resurrected. But God will catch them up to His throne, as the gleanings of the great harvest of resurrected saints; this will be the closing scene of the first resurrection. See

THE MAN CHILD

Rev. 20:4. "And I saw the souls of them that were beheaded for the witness of Jesus, and for the word of God, and which had not worshipped the beast, neither his image, neither had received his mark upon their foreheads; and they lived and reigned with Christ a thousand years." Here the martyred saints join the company heretofore resurrected, making the entire company who shall rule the nations with a rod of iron. See Rev. 2:26, 27. "And he that overcometh and keepeth my words unto the end, to him will I give power over the nations: and he shall rule them with a rod of iron; as the vessels of a potter shall they be broken to shivers."

The Woman in the Wilderness

And the woman fled into the wilderness, where she hath a place prepared of God, that they should feed her there a thousand two hundred and three-score days. And there was war in heaven: Michael and his angels fought against the dragon; and the dragon fought and his angels, and prevailed not; neither was their place found any more in heaven. And the great dragon was cast out, that old serpent, called the Devil, and Satan, which deceiveth the whole world; he was cast out into the earth, and his angels were cast out with him. And I heard a loud voice saying in heaven, Now is come salvation, and strength, and the kingdom of our God, and the power of His Christ: for the accuser of our brethren is cast down, which accused them before our God day and night. And they overcame him by the blood of the Lamb, and by the word of their testimony; and they loved not their lives unto the death. Therefore rejoice, ye heavens, and ye that dwell in them. Woe to the inhabiters of the earth and of the sea! for the devil is come down unto you, having great wrath, because he knoweth that he hath but a short time. And when the dragon saw that he was cast unto the earth, he persecuted the woman which brought forth the man-child. And to the woman were given two wings of a great eagle, that she might fly into the wilderness, into her place, where she is nourished for a time, and times, and half a time, from the face of the serpent. And the serpent cast out of his mouth water as a flood after the woman, that he might cause her to be carried away of the flood. And the earth helped the woman, and the earth opened her mouth, and swallowed up the flood which the dragon cast out of his mouth. And the dragon was wroth with the woman, and went to make war with the remnant of her seed, which keep the commandments of God and have

THE MAN CHILD

the testimony of Jesus Christ. Rev. 12:6-17.

The Church of God is often referred to as a woman, or the wife of the Lamb. The true Church of God is in heaven at this time. No mention of the church has been made since the first seal was opened. The church was suddenly and quietly removed by the Lord, as a thief in the night when the sixth seal was opened. The nominal church, as the Israelites in the wilderness in the days of Moses, were far from being holy men, but were truly selected of God, and in preparation for the future. So the 144,000 Israelites sealed by the angel in their foreheads, are now the nominal church of the future, and are removed into the wilderness, propably the same wilderness between Pales- and Egypt "Where she hath a place prepared of God that they should feed her there, a thousand two hundred and three-score days." This is the same number of days that the two witnesses prophesy, and at the same time; while the Anti-Christ army desecrates every sacred spot in Jerusalem except the temple, and altar, for forty and two months. Now the lines are clearly drawn. God has His two witnesses in the temple, and its congregation have been carried away on the "Two wings of a great eagle, that she might fly into the wilderness, into her place, where she is nourished for a time, and times, and half a time (three years and a half) from the face of the serpent," safe in the desert home, and miraculously fed by the hand of God.

War in Heaven

"And there was war in heaven." That is the heavens above this earth. This war is between Michael and his angels who always fight for Israel; and the dragon. And the dragon and his angels fought in the air above, and prevailed not, but was cast down onto the earth, and his angels with him. This dragon that was cast down is that old serpent that deceived Eve in the Garden. He is called the Devil and Satan. There is a Devil, and here he is in a desperate fight to keep God and Christ from taking this earth out of his possession, for he has held it for nearly six thousand years.

"And I heard a loud voice in heaven, saying, Now is come salvation, and strength, and the kingdom of our God, and the power of His Christ, for the accuser of our brethren is cast down, which accused them before God, day and night."

There is great rejoicing in heaven, for God has bidden them rejoice over this casting down of Satan; but woe to the inhabitants of the earth, and of the sea, for the Devil has come down to the earth having great wrath, having been defeated, and having the knowledge that he has only a short time to remain on earth before he will be shut up in the bottomless pit for a thousand years. The demons which

THE MAN CHILD 157

are in the air at the present time, will be driven down and confined to the earth, and dreadful things will occur. After Satan is cast out of heaven and down to the earth, he will turn all his venom against the 144,000 sealed Israelites, and will persecute them until God miraculously transfers them from Jerusalem to their wilderness home. When Satan finds that they are all gone, he will make war with the remnant of her seed; Israelites not sealed, who were wholly in the dark concerning the times in which they lived. They will be slaughtered on every side. Satan will also "Make war on the people which keep the commandments of God, and have the testimony of Jesus Christ."

We understand by this that the foolish virgins who were left on the earth at the first resurrection, not being ready for the coming of the Lord; and preachers and people who were then backslidden, having a form of godliness but denying the power thereof, lovers of pleasure more than lovers of God, these during the awful tribulation that came upon the earth, discovered their mistake, repented of their sins, returned to the Lord, and are at this time "keeping the commandments of God, and have the testimony of Jesus Christ." These will now suffer martyrdom at the hands of the Anti-Christ, and join the resurrected hosts in heaven. (See Revelation 15:2, 3.)

THE SEVEN-HEADED BEAST.

IT is necessary that we continually keep in mind where we are in the unfolding of the events which must come to pass. Peace which was taken from the earth has not returned. War, famine and pestilence are doing their work. The great world earthquake, the positive sign of His coming, has left the earth in ruins. The saints have been raised up to the throne in heaven to suffer no more, and the earth is left without the salt, and light, and restraint of the saints. After the saints are separated from the wicked, fire falls from heaven upon the rebellious people, upon the sea and upon the land. Demons were let loose upon the wicked for five months, but no repentance came. Then came the last great struggle of the world war. All Asia against the other parts of the world, in which the third part of men have been killed. Now the Anti-Christ, having conquered all, establishes a kingdom.

And I stood upon the sand of the sea, and saw a beast rise up out of the sea, having seven heads and ten horns, and

THE SEVEN-HEADED BEAST 159

upon his horns ten crowns, and upon his heads the name of blasphemy. And the beast which I saw was like unto a leopard, and his feet were as the feet of a bear, and his mouth as the mouth of a lion: and the dragon gave him his power, and his seat and great authority. And I saw one of his heads as it were wounded to death; and his deadly wound was healed: and all the world wondered after the beast. And they worshipped the dragon which gave power unto the beast: and they worshipped the beast, saying, Who is like unto the beast? who is able to make war with him? And there was given unto him a mouth speaking great things and blasphemies; and power was given unto him to continue forty and two months. And he opened his mouth in blasphemy against God, to blaspheme His name, and His tabernacle, and them that dwell in heaven. And it was given unto him to make war with the saints, and to overcome them; and power was given him over all kindreds, and tongues, and nations. And all that dwell upon the earth shall worship him, whose names are not written in the book of life of the Lamb slain from the foundation of the world. If any man have an ear, let him hear. Rev. 13:1-8.

"And I, John, stood on the sand of the sea,

and saw a beast rise up out of the sea." Daniel saw four beasts come up out of the sea in his vision from God, and was instructed of God that the four beasts implied four Monarchies that should arise in the earth, one after the other, and that the Babylonian monarchy was the first of the four. After that came the Media Persian, then the Grecian, and then the Roman. Daniel 7:1-8, 17, 28. So we have learned that a beast coming up out of the sea means a new kingdom. Here then is a new kingdom organized out of the sea of fighting millions of earth. This beast has seven heads. The heads direct the body. These heads probably will be seven mighty men as heads of this kingdom, or it may refer to seven kinds of monarchies confederated in this beast power.

The beast has ten horns. Horns indicate kings and governments, and this is clearly seen in this beast, as each horn is crowned. Only kings or emperors were crowns. Here we have a new kingdom, composed of ten former kingdoms coming together as one monarchy, all wearing crowns. All over the heads of this beast is labelled, "Blasphemy." This beast was like unto a leopard, spotted all over, probably indicating the different nationalities composing it. His feet were as the feet of a bear, indicating his power to tear to pieces; and his mouth as the mouth of a lion, indicating power to devour.

THE SEVEN-HEADED BEAST 161

"And the dragon gave him his power." The dragon is the Devil and Satan, that old serpent. There is a Devil and he has tremendous power, and he now gives all his power to this beast kingdom. He also gives his throne to this beast.

Satan's Throne

Satan has a throne and seat of government on this earth. In the days of John on Patmos, Satan's seat or throne was in Pergamos (Rev. 2:13), and men were dying as martyrs because of his presence and power. In these closing days Satan has his seat in Jerusalem, where the temple has been rebuilt, and there he is preparing the way for his man, the man of sin, the Antichrist. When this new kingdom of confederated nations is formed, and they have accepted the man that Satan has been using for years, or since the white horse went forth to conquer, Satan will vacate his seat or throne and will give him great authority and power. Satan will then rule the world through this man of sin, who is invested with demon power from this on.

After conquering the army of two hundred millions from Asia; subduing the world unto himself, (the third part of men having been killed in the final battles, and millions in judgment plagues), the Antichrist is finally firmly seated on the Devil's throne as Supreme Ruler. All the world will wonder at the beast, the man, and the kingdom with the supernatural unearthly power manifested, and will worship the dragon or Devil, which gave this mighty power to the beast. "And they worshipped the beast, saying, Who is like unto the beast? Who is able to make war with him?"

The Antichrist is now seated in the temple showing himself that he is God, and working signs and wonders by the power of Satan, such as was never done by man. There was given unto him a mouth speaking great things and blasphemies, and power was given unto him to do this for forty-two months. No more, no less! This is going on at the same time the two witnesses prophesy; the city is trodden down; and the church is hid, and fed in the wilderness, as already explained.

"And he opened his mouth in blasphemy against God, to blaspheme His name and his tabernacle and them that dwell in heaven. And it was given unto him to make war with the saints, and to overcome them." These saints are all persons among the Gentiles who have turned to God during the Antichrist's war of conquest; and are now living. God has saved their souls, but now permits the Antichrist to kill their bodies. This is the punishment to all who will not be ready for the coming of our King.

Repent, dear reader, and turn to God and be saved now!

THE SEVEN-HEADED BEAST 163

Power Given to the Antichrist

Power was given to the Antichrist over all kindreds, and tongues, and nations. All these shall worship the Antichrist, except the persons whose names are written in the Lamb's book of Life. All persons who truly repent of all their sins and believe on the Lord Jesus Christ, the Saviour, have their names written in this Book of Life. They will not worship the beast, and because they will not, he has them beheaded. At this time the saints must not defend themselves, for he that killeth with the sword will be killed with the sword. To take the sword would not save them. The Antichrist power now holding the sword and leading them into captivity, will in turn be taken captive by our Lord, and killed by Him. Here is the patience of the saints. They can die as martyrs, but cannot sin against God and man, by attempting to kill the Antichrist.

THE ECCLESIASTICAL BEAST

AND I beheld another beast coming up out of the earth; and he had two horns like a lamb, and he spake as a dragon. And he exerciseth all the power of the first beast before him, and causeth the earth and them which dwell therein to worship the first beast, whose deadly wound was healed. And he doeth great wonders, so that he maketh fire come down from heaven on the earth in the sight of men, and deceiveth them that dwell on the earth by the means of those miracles which he had power to do in the sight of the beast; saying to them that dwell on the earth, that they should make an image to the beast, which had the wound by a sword, and did live. And he had power to give life unto the image of the beast, that the image of the beast should both speak, and cause that as many as would not worship the image of the beast should be killed. And he causeth all, the small and the great, and the rich and the poor, and the free and the bond, that there be given them a mark on their right hand, or upon their forehead; and

THE ECCLESIASTICAL BEAST

that no man should be able to buy or to sell, save he that hath the mark, even the name of the beast or the number of his name. Here is wisdom. He that hath understanding, let him count the number of the beast; for it is the number of a man: and his number is Six Hundred and Sixty and Six. Revelation 13:11-18. R. V.

This second beast did not come up out of a sea of warring men, but came up out of the earth in quietness, unobserved as a plant growing up; but it came as surely. It had two horns, small like a lamb. It seemed perfectly harmless, but spoke as a dragon or Devil. He had all the power, and used all the powers of the first beast who came before him. This is ecclesiastical power. The Antichrist church will have a great man at its head, who will be known as a Prophet but he will be a false prophet,—the Devil's prophet. He will exercise all the power of the Beast kingdom and cause all on earth to worship the first beast, or Antichrist. Here is Church and State working hand in hand. This second Beast does great wonders, even making fire come down from heaven on the earth in the sight of men. These miraculous manifestations and signs will be wrought so as to deceive men; to deceive all *but* the children of God who know the Scriptures and know God.

Image Worship

He also commands that an image be made of the Antichrist; and when the image is completed, he gives it power to speak. Probably some mechanical, automatic contrivance is installed so that the image will move about and speak, for there will be much deception in all that he does. "He deceiveth the people."

The false prophet by Satanic power causeth that as many as would not worship the Image of the Beast should be killed (Rev. 13:15). This reminds one of the golden Image that Nebuchadnezzar set up in the plains of Dura, in Daniel's day. Again, this second beast, ecclesiastical power, causeth all, both small and great, rich and poor, slaves and masters, to receive a mark in their right hand (the one with which we do business), or in their foreheads (where it can be seen easily), and that no man might buy or sell except he that had the mark, or the name of the beast, or the number of his name. Rev. 13:16-17.

Mark of the Beast

No man has yet received the mark of the beast, nor can receive the mark until the Antichrist is on the throne, and his church is in power; and the command to go forth from the False Prophet, to mark his own true followers, so they will be known on sight, and so that those who do not hold allegiance to the Church and

THE ECCLESIASTICAL BEAST 167

the Government may be discovered: and as people must buy and sell or starve, all will be forced by hunger to show themselves. This marking will probably be tattooing into the skin with needle and ink, a mark or name or number of the beast, whatever the beast decides upon. These three forms of marking will doubtless indicate different classes of the Antichrist's followers, such as Priests, officers and subjects.

Matters become exceedingly serious for God's children of those days. Some who would not worship the image have been killed. Some have not been discovered. The drive is on to find them. The faithful ones are praying. An enforced fast is coming upon them. Food that has been scarce is running out; in some cases has run out many days since. Some have yielded and taken the mark to get bread. Some are thinking of doing so, because of the tears of wives and children. Some have actually starved to death, and many are starving. At this time no preacher dare call the saints together to encourage and strengthen them. That would expose them to sudden death which would be just what the Antichrist would rejoice in. What shall the trembling, starving, sometimes wavering saints do?

ANGELS PREACHING

AND I looked and lo, a Lamb stood on the mount Zion, and with him a hundred and forty and four thousand, having his Father's name written in their foreheads. And I heard a voice from heaven, as the voice of many waters, and as the voice of a great thunder: and I heard the voice of harpers harping with their harps: and they sung as it were a new song before the throne, and before the four beasts, and the elders: and no man could learn that song but the hundred and forty and four thousand, which were redeemed from the earth. These are they which were not defiled with women; for they are virgins. These are they which follow the Lamb whithersoever he goeth. These were redeemed from among men, being the first-fruits unto God and to the Lamb. And in their mouth was found no guile: for they are without fault before the throne of God. And I saw another angel fly in the midst of heaven, having the everlasting gospel to preach unto them that dwell on the earth, and to every nation, and kindred,

ANGELS PREACHING 169

and tongue, and people, saying with a loud voice, Fear God, and give glory to him; for the hour of his judgment is come; and worship him that made heaven, and earth, and the sea, and the fountains of waters. And there followed another angel, saying, Babylon is fallen, is fallen, that great city, because she made all nations drink of the wine of the wrath of her fornication. And the third angel followed them, saying with a loud voice, If any man worship the beast and his image, and receive his mark in his forehead, or in his hand, the same shall drink of the wine of the wrath of God, which is poured out without mixture into the cup of his indignation; and he shall be tormented with fire and brimstone in the presence of the holy angels, and in the presence of the Lamb: and the smoke of their torment ascendeth up forever and ever: and they have no rest day nor night, who worship the beast and his image, and whosoever receiveth the mark of his name. Rev. 14:1-11.

All heaven is stirred over the conditions on earth. The wavering ranks of saints must be strengthened. The devil must be defeated. "And I looked, and lo, a Lamb stood on Mount Zion, and with Him a hundred and forty and four thousand, having his Father's name written in their foreheads." Here are all the persons who came out of their graves when Jesus arose from the dead, led by their Lord, having his Father's name written in their foreheads; harping on their harps and singing the new song that none but they can sing. They are singing around the throne in heaven. It sounded like great thunder and many waters. Angels are sent out to do the preaching. Three different classes of angels follow each other in proper order, visiting each and every halting, wavering saint on earth. "Having the everlasting gospel to preach to them that dwell on the earth, and to every nation and kindred and tongue and people, saying with a loud voice, Fear God and give glory to Him; for the hour of His judgment is come: and worship Him that made heaven and earth and the sea, and the fountains of waters." That means, do not worship this devil-controlled man who says he is God.

The next angel that calls to strengthen the brethren cries out, "Babylon is fallen, is fallen, that great city, because she made all nations drink of the wine of the wrath of her fornication." All nations have been drinking ever since Cain killed his brother, and all have been drinking since the war began in 1914; but the Babylonian rule will soon be over. Its end is now being announced by angels.

"And the third angel follows, saying with a loud voice." These angels are greatly stirred and speak to stir the saints, saying, "If any man worship the beast and his image, and receive his mark in his forehead, or in his hand, the same shall drink of the wine of the wrath of God, which is poured out without mixture into the cup of His indignation; and he shall be tormented with fire and brimstone in the presence of the holy angels, and in the presence of the Lamb; and the smoke of their torment ascendeth up forever and ever, and they have no rest day nor night who worship the beast and his image, and whosoever receiveth the mark of his name." This preaching by the angels will make every saint courageous and fearless of death. At this time all the teeming millions who have, or who now take the mark of the beast and worship the image, seal their own damnation forever.

The wavering saints are strengthened, and stand firm in the faith, seeing that their suffering will soon be over; and they will enter into the "exceeding and eternal weight of glory."

They positively refuse to receive the mark; and willingly die, believing in the Lord Jesus Christ.

THE FALSE PROPHET

THE False Prophet is not the Antichrist, but will be the chief man or Ruler of the Antichrist church. He will probably be a man at the head of one of the churches on earth that can swing the largest number of men into line. He may be the Mohammedan leader or the Pope, but when he accepts the position, Satan will take full possession of him, as he did of Judas Iscariot, and he will be empowered by Satan to do signs and wonders, and to deceive the whole world.

And I heard a voice from heaven saying unto me, Write, Blessed are the dead which die in the Lord from henceforth: Yea, saith the Spirit, that they may rest from their labours; and their works do follow them. And I looked, and behold a white cloud, and upon the cloud one sat like unto the Son of Man, having on his head a golden crown, and in his hand a sharp sickle. And another angel same out of the temple, crying with a loud voice to him that sat on the cloud, Thrust in thy sickle, and reap: for the time is come for thee to reap;

THE FALSE PROPHET

for the harvest of the earth is ripe. And he that sat on the cloud thrust in his sickle on the earth; and the earth was reaped. Rev. 14:13-16.

"Blessed are the dead which die in the Lord from henceforth." The henceforth has reference to the conditions then existing. To take the mark in order to get bread and live until the end of the three and a half-year period, will mean hell, with the devil forever and ever. To refuse to take the mark is to be hunted as a rat or rabbit by dogs until destroyed. The only other alternative is to "Die in the Lord." To stand firm in the faith, washed and cleansed in the Blood of the Lamb; not counting life dear unto them; waiting patiently until death by starvation, or by being taken out of the body by the Lord, or by martyrdom; this alone will release them from a hell on earth, to the paradise above. "From henceforth," from that time on, to die in the Lord is sought for, is desired, is the most blessed thing that could come to the saints in hiding from the hosts of the Antichrist.

"And I looked, and behold a white cloud, and upon this cloud sat one like unto the Son of Man." One like unto the Son of Man, having on his head a golden crown, and in his hand a sharp sickle. John does not say that this was the Son of Man; and it seems, quite improper, that an angel should come out of the temple, crying with a loud voice to the Son of God; and commanding Him to thrust in His sickle, and reap the harvest of the earth.

This angel, who gives the command, is said to be another angel, which seems to imply that the one who sat on the white cloud with a sharp sickle in his hand, was also an angel, although he was like unto the Son of Man, and had a crown on his head.

It will be well to remember that the saints have been resurrected and caught up to be with God, on the sea of glass, before the throne; and that all the saints are now like unto the Son of Man, and wear crowns. This is God's reaper sent to gather in all the saints of that day. For the harvest of the earth is ripe; and he thrust in his sickle and the earth was reaped. Observe that this comes at the close, or near the close of the Antichrist's forty-two months' reign, while he is making his drive to exterminate all who will not worship him, and at the same time when the two witnesses fall before his mighty onslaught. All the unrepentant world rejoice that the troubles of the people, the fanatics, the heretics, the holy rollers, are gone. But God has taken them unto Himself.

The Last Overcomers.

> I saw as it were a sea of glass mingled with fire: and them that had gotten the victory over the beast, and over his image,

THE FALSE PROPHET 175

and over his mark, and over the number of his name, stand on the sea of glass, having the harps of God; and they sing the Song of Moses, the servant of God, and the Song of the Lamb, saying, Great and marvelous are thy works, Lord God Almighty; just and true are thy ways, thou King of saints. Who shall not fear thee, O Lord, and glorify thy Name? For thou only art Holy: for all nations shall come and worship before thee; for thy judgments are made manifest. Rev. 15:2-4.

Here we see all the saints who had turned to God after Jesus Christ had come and taken His own. They have gone through the great tribulation, and have refused the mark of the beast. They did not worship the beast or his image. They have overcome him by the Blood of the Lamb, and they have resisted unto blood, striving against sin. And now they are on the same sea of glass before the throne, where we saw all the saints and angels in Revelation 7:9-10, praising God. This reaping does not refer to the death of the body only. John sees the saints who refused to receive the mark, no matter how they died, in the same resurrection state, and place, as he saw the great multitude from every nation, kindred, people, and tongue who came up in the first resurrection; all standing before the throne with their harps, rejoicing and praising God. The great multitude that went up after the opening of the sixth seal knew nothing of the sorrows and tortures that had fallen upon these last overcomers, who had gotten the victory over the Antichrist, loving not their lives unto death. These are the gleanings of the harvest, and the last human beings to have part in the first resurrection.

We get another glimpse of these overcomers at the time Satan is bound and shut up in the bottomless pit for a thousand years, in Revelation 20:4.

> And I saw the souls of them that were beheaded for the witness of Jesus, and for the Word of God, and which had not worshipped the beast, neither his image, neither had received his mark upon their foreheads, or in their hands, and they lived and reigned with Christ a thousand years.

This is the Millenial reign on this earth. These had been beheaded. This will be the mode of killing under the Antichrist. These have gone through the whole of the great tribu-
came up out of the great tribulation before the lation. The great company in Revelation 7:9, Antichrist was seated on his throne.

THE DESTRUCTION OF THE WICKED

AND another angel came out of the temple which is in heaven, he also having a sharp sickle. And another angel came out from the altar, which had power over fire; and cried with a loud cry to him that had the sharp sickle, saying, Thrust in thy sharp sickle, and gather the clusters of the vine of the earth; for her grapes are fully ripe. And the angel thrust in his sickle into the earth, and gathered the vine of the earth, and cast it into the great winepress of the wrath of God. And the winepress was trodden without the city, and blood came out of the winepress, even unto the horse bridles, by the space of a thousand and six hundred furlongs. Rev. 14:17-20.

Now that God's harvest and gleaning time is over, and all the saints are gathered home, here is another reaper with a sharp sickle. He comes to reap what is left after the saints are all gone. For they are fully ripe; ripe in sin, and ripe for destruction. They are cast into "the great winepress of the wrath of God," and the winepress was trodden without the city, and blood came out of the winepress, even unto the horse bridles, by the space of a thousand and six hundred furlongs. Here is a stream of blood that indicates the destruction of hundreds of millions of human beings, cast into the great winepress of the wrath of God: men who have become desperately wicked; men who defy God to His face, and curse Him; men who will not be saved.

When the Lord Jesus shall be revealed from heaven with His mighty angels in flaming fire, taking vengeance on them that know not God, and that obey not the gospel of our Lord Jesus Christ: who shall be punished with everlasting destruction from the presence of the Lord, and from the glory of His power; when He shall come to be glorified in His saints, and to be admired in all them that believe in that day. 2 Thes. 1:7-10.

THE SEVEN LAST PLAGUES.

AND I saw another sign in heaven, great and marvellous, seven angels having the seven last plagues; for in them is filled up the wrath of God. And I saw as it were a sea of glass mingled with fire: and them that has gotten the victory over the beast, and over his image, and over his mark, and over the number of his name, stand on the sea of glass, having the harps of God. And they sing the Song of Moses the servant of God, and the Song of the Lamb, saying, Great and marvellous are thy works, Lord God Almighty; just and true are thy ways, thou King of saints. Who shall not fear thee, O Lord, and glorify thy name? for thou only art holy: for all nations shall come and worship before thee; for thy judgments are made manifest. And after that I looked, and, behold, the temple of the tabernacle of the testimony in heaven was opened: And the seven angels came out of the temple, having the seven plagues, clothed in pure and white linen, and having their breasts girded with golden girdles. And one of the four beasts gave unto the seven angels seven golden vials full of the wrath of God, who liveth forever and ever. And the temple was filled with smoke from the glory of God, and from his power; and no man was able to enter into the temple till the seven plagues of the seven angels were fulfilled. Rev. 15:1-8.

The seven angels with the seven vials filled with the wrath of God, now come to do their work. The saints who had gotten the victory over the Antichrist are before the throne in heaven, having the harps of God, resurrected and glorified, and singing the song of Moses and the song of the Lamb. Two songs! Deliverance from the Antichrist, and cleansing by the blood of the Lamb! Now that the saints are all gathered off the earth, an angel is sent to reap the haters of God, and cleanse the earth, restoring all things, that the earth may have her sabbath, and Christ and His saints may reign during the seven-thousandth year. The seven angels having the seven last plagues are clothed in pure white linen, having their breasts girded with golden girdles. They go forth to slay men. Their white robes and golden girdles indicate that this slaying of men is righteous judgment upon men who have persistently defied God, and destroyed God's people from the earth. Observe that these are the *seven last plagues*. We are rapidly nearing the close of this great tragedy.

THE SEVEN PLAGUES

Full of the Wrath of God

"And one of the four living creatures at the throne gave unto the seven angels seven golden bowls full of the wrath of God who liveth forever and ever." O, think of the wrath of God! Who can stand before the wrath of God?

"And the temple was filled with smoke from the glory of God and from His power and no man was able to enter into the temple till the seven plagues of the seven angels were fulfilled." The temple was open at this time as the angels came out, but no man can enter into the temple in heaven until God finishes His work on earth, dealing with sin and putting down rebellion.

And I heard a great voice out of the temple saying to the seven angels, Go your ways, and pour out the vials of the wrath of God upon the earth. And the first went, and poured out his vial upon the earth; and there fell a noisome and grievous sore upon the men which had the mark of the beast, and upon them which worshipped his image. And the second angel poured out his vial upon the sea; and it became as the blood of a dead man; and every living soul died in the sea. And the third angel poured out his vial upon the rivers and fountains of waters; and they became blood. And I heard the angel of the waters say, Thou art righteous, O Lord, which art, and wast, and shalt be, because thou hast judged thus. For they have shed the blood of saints and prophets, and thou hast given them blood to drink; for they are worthy. And I heard another out of the altar say, Even so, Lord God Almighty, true and righteous are thy judgments. And the fourth angel poured out his vial upon the sun; and power was given unto him to scorch men with fire. And men were scorched with great heat, and blasphemed the name of God, which hath power over these plagues: and they repented not to give Him glory. Rev. 16:1-9.

A great voice from God, "Go your ways," and the first bowl was poured out. "And there fell a noisome and grievous sore upon the men which had the mark of the beast, and upon them which worshipped his image." This grievous sore will probably be similar to the sore that fell upon Job, causing him such anguish. And it fell upon the men who had the mark of the beast.

"And the second angel poured out his bowl upon the sea; and the sea became as the blood of a dead man." That would be stagnant blood so that every living creature in the sea died. Under the sounding of the second trumpet, the third part of the sea turned to blood, and the third part of the creatures in the sea died. Now

THE SEVEN PLAGUES 183

all the sea becomes stagnated blood, and every remaining living creature dies. Can you grasp such a scene as the oceans turned into stagnant blood, full of dead carcasses of all things that had lived in the sea?

"And the third angel poured out his bowl upon the rivers and lakes, and fountains of fresh waters, and they became blood." God turned all the waters of Egypt into blood in the days of Moses (Genesis 7:19-20), now He turns all fresh water on earth into blood.

"And I heard the angel of the waters say, Thou art righteous, O Lord, which art, and wast, and shall be, because thou hast judged thus. For they have shed the blood of saints and prophets, and thou hast given them blood to drink, for they are worthy." This was said of the men who had killed all the saints on earth of that time, and God's wrath in giving them blood to drink is commended as a righteous punishment.

"And the fourth angel poured out his bowl upon the sun, and the sun scorched men with fire." Dreadful suffering will result from this plague, bringing death; yet the earth dwellers upon being scorched by the sun, blasphemed the name of God and repented not of their sins, nor asked forgiveness of God.

And the fifth angel poured out his vial upon the seat of the beast; and his kingdom was full of darkness; and they gnawed their tongues for pain, and blasphemed the God of heaven because of their pains and their sores, and repented not of their deeds. And the sixth angel poured out his vial upon the great river Euphrates; and the water thereof was dried up, that the way of the kings of the East might be prepared. And I saw three unclean spirits, like frogs, come out of the mouth of the dragon, and out of the mouth of the beast, and out of the mouth of the false prophet. For they are the spirits of devils, working miracles, which go forth unto the kings of the earth and of the whole world, to gather them to the battle of that great day of God Almighty. Behold, I come as a thief. Blessed is he that watcheth, and keepeth his garments, lest he walk naked, and they see his shame. And he gathered them together into a place called in the Hebrew tongue Armageddon. And the seventh angel poured out his vial into the air; and there came a great voice out of the temple of heaven, from the throne, saying, It is done. And there were voices, and thunders, and lightnings; and there was a great earthquake, such as was not since men were upon the earth, so mighty an earthquake, and so great. And the great city was divided into three parts, and the cities of the nations fell: and great Babylon came

THE SEVEN PLAGUES

in remembrance before God, to give unto her the cup of the wine of the fierceness of his wrath. And every island fled away, and the mountains were not found. And there fell upon men a great hail out of heaven, every stone about the weight of a talent: and men blasphemed God because of the plague of the hail; for the plague thereof was exceeding great. Rev. 16:10-21.

What an awful condition the people are now in. A noisome and grievous sore breaks out on their bodies. The seas are full of rottenness and stench fills the air. Only blood to drink, the sun scorching them, and the heat smothering them. And they gnawed their tongues for pain. In all this we see there is no repentance, no turning from sin, no asking for mercy. These are all demon-possessed people, who sold themselves, soul and body, to the devil when they took the mark of the beast and worshipped the Antichrist, the Man of Sin.

"And the sixth angel poured out his bowl upon the great river Euphrates." And the waters of the river were dried up so armies from the east could pass over to Jerusalem to the great closing battle of God Almighty. And the demon spirits went forth from Satan, and from the Antichrist, and from the false prophet, to deceive the Kings of the Earth, and gather them to the place of final destruction. And they were gathered into a place called Armageddon.

"And the seventh angel poured out his bowl into the air, and there came a great voice out of the temple in heaven, from the throne, saying, It is done."

All these are facts. No fiction here. The seven last plagues have been poured out and men are dead and dying on every side, but will not yield to God; will not repent.

Last Earthquake

"And there were voices, and thunderings, and lightnings, and there was a great earthquake, such as was not since men were upon the earth, so mighty an earthquake and so great."

This roar of voices and power was from God. And every Island fled away, and the mountains disappeared, probably sank back, or down, from whence they had been upheaved when sin first came into the world. The earth shall again become a plain. Another earthquake, "Such as was not since men were upon the earth, so mighty an earthquake, and so great."

When the sixth seal was opened, there was an earthquake that moved every island and every mountain out of their places. A world earthquake. When the last of "the seven last plagues" was poured out, this greatest earthquake that ever was since man was upon the earth, occurs. And every island fled away, and every mountain disappeared. A second time the whole world is laid waste. Man's attempt to rebuild the earth after the first terrible earthquake, is thwarted. All is again lying in ruins. All "The Cities of the nations fell; and great Babylon came in remembrance before God, to give unto her the cup of the wine of the fierceness of His wrath." And Jerusalem was divided into three parts. And there fell upon men a great hail out of heaven, each stone about the weight of a talent. And men continued to blaspheme God because of the plague of the hail, for the plague thereof was exceeding great. All these plagues and suffering fail to bring men to repentance; there was no turning to God. How desperately wicked men have become in these last days. All of this is just ahead of us and soon will be enacted in this great world drama. This generation will not pass away until all these things are fulfilled. "Behold I come as a thief, blessed is he that watcheth and keepeth his garments, lest he walk naked and they see his shame."

As a result of this earthquake the city of Jerusalem will be divided into three parts, and all the cities of the different nations will fall. Heaven and earth will shake and tremble before the wrath of an angry God, but wicked men will curse on.

"And Babylon came in remembrance before God to give unto her the cup of the wine of the fierceness of His wrath." Fiercer wrath than has yet been seen will soon fall on Babylon. God cannot lie; all these statements are facts. The scarlet-colored beast is not present at this time but will, at the appointed time, supplant the leopard beast now in existence. We are nearing the close of the time of the leopard beast, and the appearing of the scarlet-colored beast mentioned in Revelation 17, who is an eighth, but is of the seventh beast. All men now carry the mark of the beast, having killed all who would not receive the mark, and worship the image. And God has sent forth the seven angels to pour out the last seven plagues upon them.

THE SCARLET-COLORED BEAST.

AND there came one of the seven angels that had the seven bowls, and spake with me, saying, Come hither, I will shew thee the judgment of the great harlot that sitteth upon many waters; with whom the kings of the earth committed fornication, and they that dwell in the earth were made drunken with the wine of her fornication. And he carried me away in the Spirit into a wilderness: and I saw a woman sitting upon a scarlet-colored beast, full of names of blasphemy, having seven heads and ten horns. And the woman was arrayed in purple and scarlet, and decked with gold and precious stone and pearls, having in her hand a golden cup full of abominations, even the unclean things of her fornication, and upon her forehead a name written, Mystery, Babylon the Great, the mother of the harlots and of the abominations of the earth. And I saw the woman drunken with the blood of the saints, and with the blood of the martyrs of Jesus. And when I saw her, I wondered with a great wonder. And the angel said unto me, Wherefore didst thou wonder? I will tell thee the mystery of the woman, and of the beast that carrieth her, which hath the seven heads and the ten horns. The beast that thou sawest was, and is not; and is about to come up out of the abyss, and to go into perdition. And they that dwell on the earth shall wonder, they whose name hath not been written in the book of life from the foundation of the world, when they behold the beast, how that he was, and is not, and shall come. Here is the mind that hath wisdom. The seven heads are seven mountains, on which the woman sitteth: and they are seven kings; the five are fallen, the one is, the other is not yet come; and when he cometh, he must continue a little while. And the beast that was, and is not, is himself also an eighth, and is of the seven; and he goeth into perdition. And the ten horns that thou sawest are ten kings, who have received no kingdom as yet; but they receive authority as kings, with the beast, for one hour. These have one mind, and they give their power and authority unto the beast. These shall war against the Lamb, and the Lamb shall overcome them, for he is Lord of lords, and King of kings; and they also shall overcome that are with him, called and chosen and faithful. And he saith unto me, the waters which thou sawest, where

THE SCARLET-COLORED BEAST 191

the harlot sitteth, are peoples, and multitudes, and nations, and tongues. And the ten horns which thou sawest, and the beast, these shall hate the harlot, and shall make her desolate and naked, and shall eat her flesh, and shall burn her utterly with fire. For God did put in their hearts to do his mind, and to come to one mind, and to give their kingdom unto the beast, until the words of God should be accomplished. And the woman whom thou sawest is the great city, which reigneth over the kings of the earth. Rev. 17:1-18. R. V.

The destruction of Babylon is the closing scene in this whole work of destroying them that destroy the earth. "In her (Babylon), was found the blood of prophets and of saints and of all that were slain upon the earth." Rev. 18:24.

If a great city should be built upon the ancient site of old Babylon, and that city duplicated in all points and particulars, to be destroyed at the proper time, could it be truthfully said of the one thus built, that "In it was found the blood of prophets, and saints and of all that were slain upon the earth?" Or if the Roman Catholic Church should be annihilated, and the City of Rome also, could it be truthfully said that in them had been found the blood of all that had been slain on earth? God, who cannot lie, declares that in the Babylon we are about to consider; when it is destroyed, there will be found in it, "The blood of prophets and of saints, and of all that were slain upon the earth." *THIS BABYLON* is the source, the fountain-head, the producer, the mother of all the abominations on the earth, as well as the mother of harlots.

Here we have another Beast, a scarlet-colored beast, full of names of blasphemy, having seven heads and ten horns. As John marvelled, the angel said unto him, "Why didst thou marvel? I will tell thee the mystery of the woman and of the beast that carrieth her, which hath the seven heads and ten horns." Then there is a mystery about this woman, and beast.

The beast that thou sawest was, and is not now in existence: there is a beast kingdom in existence, but John is shown another beast that is not, and it, when it comes, shall ascend out of the bottomless pit, and when it departs, it will go back into perdition. This beast was, and is not, and yet is. This scarlet-colored beast is of Satanic origin. It comes up out of the bottomless pit; and will go back there. The ecclesiastical beast is said to have come up out of the earth. The bottomless pit is in the heart of this earth. The scarlet-colored beast is an eighth beast, and is of the seventh beast; that is, the seventh beast produced the eighth.

THE SCARLET-COLORED BEAST 193

Seven Kingdoms

There are seven kingdoms, five of them are fallen, one is now in existence, and the other is not yet come; and when he cometh he must continue a short space. Here are the seven beasts indicated by the seven heads of the beast. Five of these seven are fallen: the Babylonian, the Medo-Persian, the Greek, the Roman, and the ten-toe condition of the fourth beast down to the time of the Antichrist's seven-headed confederacy, which was then in existence, being the sixth beast with its ecclesiastical Beast, which is the seventh. And the beast which was, and is not, even he is the eighth, and is of the seventh (ecclesiastical), and with it will go into perdition and shall not be perpetuated. Here is a clear statement of facts that show us that the beast the woman sat on was not yet in existence, but would come as the last beast, an eighth, but was of the seventh. A change of government brought about by the Antichrist Church.

This scarlet-colored beast will not come into existence by revolution among the people, but by intrigue in the ecclesiastical, two-horned beast power, and by the capitalists of that day under the mighty power of Satan and the Man of Sin, the Antichrist. As a result of this, capital will completely dominate and crush the people. This scarlet-colored beast was full of names of blasphemy, having ten horns, but no crowns. The sixth beast was like unto a leopard having ten horns and ten crowns. The ten horns on this last scarlet-colored beast are ten kings, which have received no kingdom as yet, but receive power as kings one hour with the beast, Anti-Christ. They have one mind and will give their power to the beast. They will make war with the Lamb, and the Lamb will overcome them.

Here we find the same confederacy of ten horns (nations) with the former ten kings discarded, and ten other men who never had been kings put in their places. This beast was scarlet-colored with the blood of the saints they had killed. The woman was seated on this beast. She was in the saddle with reins in hand, guiding the beast. The woman is a prostitute and is sitting upon many waters. "And the waters which thou sawest, where the whore sitteth, are peoples, and multitudes and nations and tongues." This vile woman was sitting upon all the people on earth. The Roman Catholic Church never did this. Babylon, if rebuilt, would not do this, but God says this woman was sitting on all the people on earth. Who can this be, what can this be, that is sitting on all the people, and will, in the closing days of the Antichrist Kingdom, sit in the saddle? The kings of the earth have committed fornication with this woman, they have sought after her, and sinned with her; but the kings of the earth never sought after the Catholic Church. The inhabitants of the earth have been made drunk with the wine of her for-

THE SCARLET-COLORED BEAST 195

nication. This is not true of the Catholic Church. Most of the inhabitants of the earth know almost nothing of the Catholic Church.

Abominations of the Earth

The woman was arrayed in purple and scarlet color and decked with gold and precious stones and pearls, having a golden cup in her hand full of abominations and filthiness of her fornications. This description implies great wealth. The people of the Catholic Church are poor people the world over, so this woman could not represent the Catholic Church, or any other church on earth. Upon her forehead was a name written, "MYSTERY, BABYLON THE GREAT, THE MOTHER OF HARLOTS AND ABOMINATIONS OF THE EARTH," the mother of all crime, all impurity, all wars, all drunkenness, all gambling, all bribery, all murder, all theft, all injustice, all intrigues, all national corruption, all Legislative corruption, all Court corruption, all business corruption, all church corruption, all the abominations of the earth.

"The love of money is the root of all evil." I Timothy 6:10. This woman is the mother of all the abominations. As the tree and its fruit comes from the root, and as children come from the mother, so all the abominations known among men come from that accursed thing called GREED, covetousness, wanting what the other man has. It was this desire to have all, in Cain, that caused him to put his only brother to death, so that he might receive the blessing that came from God to Abel. The first human blood was shed by this woman, and all blood shed ever since, has been to get some advantage over his brother man. This woman is COMMERCIALISM. This word is used to imply doing business, buying, selling, trading or trafficking for profit. All strifes, whether national or individual, in court or on the street, with the fist or with the gun, with the tongue or with the torpedo, in the pulpit or the newspaper, are fought to get gain.

The ten kings that were at the heads of the ten nations that confederated under the Antichrist, will be set aside by him after he is firmly established as God Almighty, and ten men, not kings, put in their places to reign for the little time still remaining of the forty-two months. These ten kings shall be of one mind and shall give their power and strength unto the Antichrist. These ten kings and the Antichrist shall make war with the Lamb and the Lamb shall overcome them.

Woman Drunken

"And I saw the woman drunken with the blood of the saints, and with the blood of the martyrs of Jesus." This implies that capitalism had much to do with, if not wholly responsible

THE SCARLET-COLORED BEAST 197

for, the slaughter of the saints. "And the ten horns which thou sawest upon the beast, these shall hate the whore and shall make her desolate and naked, and shall eat her flesh and burn her with fire. For God hath put in their hearts to fulfil his will, and to agree, and give their kingdom unto the beast, until the words of God shall be fulfilled." When Commercialism is drunk over its success in getting into the national saddle, and riding over its victims, the people will arise in resentment; and when the ten kings lead them in their resistance, with God urging them on, terrible things will take place. The angel tells John that this woman is that "Great City which reigneth over the kings of the earth."

The Anti-Christ, after having marked all of his willing, faithful, loyal followers, so that they may be known on sight, discovers many who have not taken the mark and who do not worship him. Therefore, the scarlet-colored beast and the woman in the saddle, when they come, together with the Antichrist, will fix a day after which no man who has not taken the mark and fallen down to worship the beast and his image, can buy food or other necessities. These will be dreadful days. To take the mark and worship the beast brings eternal damnation, and to refuse to take the mark brings starvation or martyrdom.

> And after these things I saw another angel come down from heaven, having

great power; and the earth was lightened with his glory. And he cried mightily with a strong voice, saying, Babylon the Great is fallen, is fallen, and is become the habitation of devils, and the hold of every foul spirit, and a cage of every unclean and hateful bird. For all nations have drunk of the wine of the wrath of her fornication, and the kings of the earth have committed fornication with her, and the merchants of the earth are waxed rich through the abundance of her delicacies. Rev. 18:1-3.

Babylon or Commercialism, at this time, has become the habitation of demons, and the stronghold, or fortified home, of every foul and unclean, hateful person of big business and trickery. Because of advantage, all the kings of the earth have committed fornication with commercialism, joining in with their schemes to gain wealth and obtain advantage over others. The merchants of the earth have become rich by standing in with them. All nations have been compelled to drink of the evil consequences of their doings, in amassing wealth.

This is not true of any church on earth, but it is true of Commercialism. All the crooks and gamblers and saloonkeepers and owners of resorts, dives, brothels, shows, theaters, and dance halls, are in with capitalism, and capitalism stands in with them; they are all after the money. Demon spirits control all of them.

THE SCARLET-COLORED BEAST 199

Bribery is little known among the poor, but is rampant among the moneyed class, corrupting every one it touches in church and state. All wickedness is found in Babylon and in Commercialism. Babylon never represented confusion of religious doctrines, never did it represent piety or religion; but it did, and does represent Gold and its worship. We have the "Image" of Commercialism in Babylon with a "head of fine gold, his breast and his arms of silver, his belly and thighs of brass, his legs of iron, his feet part of iron, and part of clay." Dan. 2:32-33. And Daniel said to the King of Babylon, "Thou art this head of gold." In this image we find gold, silver, brass, iron and clay. In these lie the wealth of the world, and Babylon stood, and stands for these.

Babylon was the head of gold, and worshipped gold, and had an image of gold set up to worship, in the plains of Dura. See Dan. 3:1-6. "Nebuchadnezzar, the king, made an image of gold, whose height was three score cubits, and the breadth thereof six cubits: he set it up in the plain of Dura, in the province of Babylon. Then Nebuchadnezzar, the king, sent to gather together the princes, the governors, and the captains, the judges, the treasurers, the counsellors, the sheriffs, and all the rulers of the provinces, to come to the dedication of the image which Nebuchadnezzar, the king, had set up. Then the princess, the governors, and captains, the judges, the treasurers, the counsellors, the sheriffs, and all the rulers of the provinces, were gathered together unto the dedication of the image that Nebuchadnezzar had set up. Then an herald cried aloud, To you it is commanded, O people, nations, and languages, That at what time ye hear the sound of the cornet, flute, harp, sackbut, psaltery, dulcimer, and all kinds of musick, ye fall down and worship the golden image that Nebuchadnezzar, the king, hath set up: And whoso falleth not down and worshippeth shall the same hour be cast into the midst of a burning fiery furnace."

Here is Commercialism full-fledged, and in the very act of worshipping the great golden image. Babylon is, and stands for gold, and the treasures of wealth; silver, brass, iron, and earthenware, including glass and all minerals. Are not these metals and minerals the things that capitalism is after continually? "All nations have drunk of the wine of the wrath of her fornication." Have suffered because of the manipulations of money and mines and business. "And the kings of the earth have committed fornication with her." They have entered into schemes with commercialism for a share of the money to be made out of the schemes, backing up commercialism with army and navy. "And the merchants of the earth are waxed rich through the abundance of her delicacies," (not religion).

And I heard another voice from heaven, saying, Come out of her, my people, that ye be not partakers of her sins, and that ye receive not of her plagues. For her sins have reached unto heaven, and God hath remembered her iniquities. Reward her even as she rewarded you, and double unto her double according to her works: in the cup which she hath filled fill to her double. How much she hath glorified herself, and lived deliciously, so much torment and sorrow give her: for she saith in her heart, I sit a queen, and and am no widow, and shall see no sorrow. Therefore shall her plagues come in one day, death, and mourning and famine; and she shall be utterly burned with fire: for strong is the Lord God who judgeth her. Rev. 18:4-8.

Many of God's children have been drawn into Commercialism in these last days, and have lost all spiritual life. They have become defiled by her filthiness in business methods; have grieved the Holy Spirit; finally quenched the Spirit. This class of persons are here called to come out of the unholy alliance, "Wherefore come out from among them, and be ye separate, saith the Lord, and touch not the unclean thing, and I will receive you, and will be a father unto you, and ye shall be my sons and daughters, saith the Lord Almighty." 2 Cor. 6:17-18. If they remain in the unholy alliance or relationship, they continue to be a partaker of her sins; and when the destruction comes to Babylon, they too shall be partakers of her plagues.

It is commonly conceded that a man cannot succeed in business these days and be a Christian. He must stoop to the trickery of the trade, or fail in his business. Come out from among them, and save your soul. If your heart is set on riches, you are an idolater. If you are practicing deceit you are not fit for the kingdom. If you have laid up treasures on earth, your heart is with them, and not with God. "COME OUT OF HER, MY PEOPLE."

The scarlet-colored beast is now in existence, and in full control of everything. The Anti-Christ and the capitalists of the whole earth are ruling all, and sitting on the people of all nations, peoples, multitudes and tongues.

> And the kings of the earth, who have committed fornication and lived deliciously with her, shall bewail her, and lament for her, when they shall see the smoke of her burning, Standing afar off for the fear of her torment, saying, Alas, alas, that great city, Babylon, that mighty city; for in one hour is thy judgment come. And the merchants of the earth shall weep and mourn over her; for no man buyeth their merchandise any more: the merchandise of gold, and silver, and precious stones, and of

THE SCARLET-COLORED BEAST 203

pearls, and fine linen, and purple, and silk, and scarlet, and all thyine wood, and all manner vessels of ivory, and all manner vessels of most precious wood, and of brass, and iron, and marble, and cinnamon, and odours, and ointments, and frankincense, and wine, and oil, and fine flour, and wheat, and beasts, and sheep, and horses, and chariots, and slaves, and souls of men. And the fruits that thy soul lusted after are departed from thee, and all things which were dainty and goodly are departed from thee, and thou shalt find them no more at all.

The merchants of these things, which were made rich by her, shall stand afar off for the fear of her torment, weeping and wailing, and saying, Alas, alas, that great city, that was clothed in fine linen, and purple, and scarlet, and decked with gold, and precious stones, and pearls! For in one hour so great riches is come to nought. And every shipmaster, and all the company in ships, and sailors, and as many as trade by sea, stood afar off, and cried when they saw the smoke of her burning, saying, What city is like unto this great city! And they cast dust on their heads, and cried, weeping and wailing, saying, Alas, alas, that great city, wherein were made rich all that had ships in the sea by reason of her costliness! For in one hour is she made desolate. Rev. 18:9-19.

The kings of the earth who have been made rich by commercialism, and have retired to roll in luxury, although now set aside by the Antichrist, bewail and lament for her, "When they see the smoke of her burning, standing afar off, for the fear of her torment, saying, Alas, alas, that great city, Babylon, that mighty city, for in one hour is thy judgment come."

"And the merchants of the earth shall weep and mourn over her, for no man buyeth their merchandise any more." The retired kings and merchants would not be so distressed over the destruction of the Catholic Church, or all the churches on earth. That is not what they are crying about. It is their source of wealth that has been struck, and causing their concern. "The merchants which were made rich by her, shall stand afar off for fear of her torment, weeping and wailing, for in one hour so great riches is come to nought." The merchants of the earth have not been made rich by any of the churches, and they only care for the churches so far as they can make money out of them. "And every shipmaster, and all the company of ships and sailors and as many as trade by sea, stood afar off" crying in distress, not over some calamity that has struck the church, or churches, but over the calamity that has struck their business, bringing their great riches to nought.

THE SCARLET-COLORED BEAST 205

Many ministers who have become rich "Eating the fat and clothing themselves with the wool" (read Ezekiel 34:1-10), have become partners in this iniquity and will wail also when Babylon is destroyed.

> Rejoice over her, thou heaven, and ye holy apostles and prophets; for God hath avenged you on her. And a mighty angel took up a stone like a great millstone, and cast it into the sea, saying, Thus with violence shall that great city, Babylon, be thrown down, and shall be found no more at all. And the voice of harpers, and musicians, and of pipers, and trumpeters, shall be heard no more at all in thee; and no craftsman, of whatsoever craft he be, shall be found any more in thee; and the sound of a millstone shall be heard no more at all in thee; and the light of a candle shall shine no more at all in thee; and the voice of the bridegroom and of the bride shall be heard no more at all in thee; for thy merchants were the great men of the earth: for by thy sorceries were all nations deceived. And in her was found the blood of prophets, and of saints, and of all that were slain upon the earth. Rev. 18:20-24.

No more shall one class of men prey upon the other class. No more shall commercialism fatten and live in ease off the sweat and tears and blood of their fellowmen, and women, and children. "For by thy sorceries were all nations deceived." This is that mysterious, sorcery working, filthy woman that had corrupted kings and courts, people and churches everywhere, and made all the world drink of the wine of her fornication in every age since Cain killed Abel, to get his place and blessing. Upon the woman's head was a name, "Mystery." This is the mystery: how one man (by financial manipulations, often by the meanest trickery), can come into possession of millions of money that had been brought into existence through the labors of tens of thousands of people who die in poverty. Her golden cup is full of her filthiness. The greed for gold turns the hearts of men into stone; makes their conscience steel.

"And in her was found the blood of prophets, and of saints, and of all that were slain upon the earth." This could not be truthfully said of any person, organization, or thing on earth except Commercialism. God commands all heaven, and the holy apostles and prophets to rejoice over the destruction of Babylon, declaring that "God hath avenged you on her." Babylon, Commercialism, has damaged, defiled, and been a curse to God's children in all ages. It kills out all spirituality wherever it goes, and it goes into the pews, even the pulpits, to strangle the people of God. It is the devil's greatest agent for the destruction of men. The

THE SCARLET-COLORED BEAST 207

devil held up commercialism in all its attractiveness before the mind of Jesus, saying, "All this will I give thee if thou wilt worship me." The man who worships wealth, worships the devil, and loses his own soul.

There could be no millenium on earth with Commercialism in existence. No more big business, no more amassing of wealth. When the Holy Ghost fell on, and filled the one hundred and twenty, on the day of Pentecost; and thousands of other converts were baptized with the Holy Ghost, they sold their possessions; and laid the money at the apostles' feet; and distribution of the funds was made, so no man lacked anything. When Christ reigns on earth, and the greed for gain is dead and gone, men will learn wisdom. We never can have peace on earth, and good will to men, with Commercialism in existence.

> Go to now, ye rich men, weep and howl for your miseries that shall come upon you. Your riches are corrupted, and your garments are moth-eaten. Your gold and silver is cankered; and the rust of them shall be a witness against you, and shall eat your flesh as it were fire. Ye have heaped treasure together for the last days. Behold, the hire of the labourers who have reaped down your fields, which is of you kept back by fraud, crieth: and the cries of them

which have reaped are entered into the ears of the Lord of sabaoth. Ye have lived in pleasure on the earth, and been wanton; ye have nourished your hearts, as in the day of slaughter. James 5:1-5.

These are facts, not fiction. Will you believe God? He is telling you the truth. These things are all coming to pass, and coming very soon. We believe that this generation will not pass away until all this comes to pass.

THE MARRIAGE OF THE LAMB

AND after these things I heard a great voice of much people in heaven, saying, Alleluia: Salvation, and glory, and honour, and power, unto the Lord our God: for true and righteous are his judgments: for he hath judged the great whore, which did corrupt the earth with her fornication, and hath avenged the blood of his servants at her hand. And again they said, Alleluia. And her smoke rose up forever and ever, and the four and twenty elders and the four beasts fell down and worshipped God that sat on the throne, saying, Amen; Alleluia. And a voice came out of the throne, saying, Praise our God, all ye his servants, and ye that fear him, both small and great. And I heard as it were the voice of a great multitude, and as the voice of many waters, and as the voice of mighty thunderings, saying Alleluia: for the Lord God omnipotent reigneth. Let us be glad and rejoice, and give honour to him: for the marriage of the Lamb is come, and his wife hath made herself ready. And to her was granted that she should be arrayed in fine linen, clean and white: for the fine linen is the righteousness of saints. And he saith unto me, Write, Blessed are they which are called unto the marriage supper of the Lamb. And he saith unto me, These are the true sayings of God. Rev. 19:1-9.

"And after these things." After the actual destruction of Babylon with its scenes of woe and wailing, a great voice of rejoicing is heard in heaven, praising God for having judged and destroyed the great whore which had corrupted the whole earth with her fornication. This shows clearly that the resurrected saints in heaven, know what is being done on earth, and praise God as they see sin and sinners, and all wickedness being removed from the earth that Christ may reign here in righteousness for a thousand years.

"For the Lord God omnipotent reigneth. Let us be glad and rejoice and give honour to Him: for the marriage of the Lamb is come, and his wife hath made herself ready." Here is the marriage of the Lamb. It comes after Babylon is destroyed and as a celebration of that event. All heaven will sing, when commercial tyranny is no more, when men will live as brethren and walk by the golden rule.

The resurrected saints in heaven—not in the air, but in heaven, while the Antichrist is still on earth—appear in fine linen, clean and white. This fine linen is the righteousness of saints. Sin

THE MARRIAGE OF THE LAMB 211

had all been eradicated and the saints were righteous, pure, holy, whiter than snow. Christ had finished His work in them, making them pure as He, Christ, is pure. (See 1 John 3:3.

"And he said unto me, These are the true sayings of God." All the book of Revelation is the true sayings of God. No fiction here. All are *facts, facts, facts: "Things that must shortly come to pass."* "And he said unto me, Write, Blessed are they which are called unto the marriage of the Lamb." This call was to be sounded out in every nation on earth. Many are called, and all who will may come; but few are chosen, because they will not go on to perfection. YOU have been called: Will *you* now give all diligence to make your calling and election sure? "Be ye holy for I am holy," is the requirement. "For without holiness no man shall see the Lord." Here are the holy ones at the Marriage in heaven just before the descent of our Lord to the earth with all the saints to destroy the Antichrist and take the Kingdom.

"And I fell at his feet to worship him. And he said unto me, see thou do it not: I am thy fellow-servant ,and of thy brethren that have the testimony of Jesus: worship God: for the testimony of Jesus is the spirit of prophecy." Rev. 19:10. John, overwhelmed with the glory of that scene and the presence of the one who had spoken unto him, fell at his feet to worship him, supposing that he was God. We have here the best view given in the Scriptures of what we will be in the resurrected state. This was a human being with the glorified body like unto Christ's glorious body. "We shall be like Him for we shall see Him as He is." John thought that this person was God.

And I saw heaven opened, and behold a white horse; and he that sat upon him was called Faithful and True, and in righteousness he doth judge and make war. His eyes were as a flame of fire, and on his head were many crowns; and he had a name written, that no man knew, but he himself. And he was clothed with a vesture dipped in blood: and his name is called THE WORD OF GOD. And the armies which were in heaven followed him upon white horses, clothed in fine linen, white and clean. And out of his mouth goeth a sharp sword, that with it he should smite the nations: and he shall rule them with a rod of iron: and he treadeth the winepress of the fierceness and wrath of Almighty God. And he hath on his vesture and on his thigh a name written, KING OF KINGS AND LORD OF LORDS. Rev. 19:11-16.

This is a description of the wonderful Christ, as He rides out of heaven on a white horse with many crowns on His head, followed by the

THE MARRIAGE OF THE LAMB 213

armies of heaven; all the holy angels, and all the saints, in His descent to earth to take the Kingdom. All His army is clothed in "fine linen, white and clean." He comes to smite the nations and rule them with a rod of iron. "And as the vessels of a potter shall they be broken to shivers." Rev. 2:27. "And He treadeth the winepress of the fierceness and wrath of Almighty God." He is King of kings, and Lord of lords.

And I saw an angel standing in the sun; and he cried with a loud voice, saying to all the fowls that fly in the midst of heaven, Come and gather yourselves together unto the supper of the great God; that ye may eat the flesh of kings, and the flesh of captains, and the flesh of mighty men, and the flesh of horses, and of them that sit on them, and the flesh of all men, both free and bond, both small and great. And I saw the beast, and the kings of the earth, and their armies, gathered together to make war against him that sat on the horse, and against his army. And the beast was taken, and with him the false prophet that wrought miracles before him, with which he deceived them that had received the mark of the beast, and them that worshipped his image. These both were cast alive into a lake of fire burning with brimstone. And the remnant were slain with the sword of him that sat upon the horse, which sword proceeded out of his mouth: and all the fowls were filled wtih their flesh. Rev. 19:17-21.

No man can comprehend the awfulness of this last closing scene of destruction. Before it commences, all the fowls that fly in the midst of heaven (the heaven above this earth) are summoned to come and gather themselves together unto the Supper of the Great God, that they may eat the flesh of kings, and the flesh of captains, and the flesh of mighty men, and the flesh of horses, and them that sit on them, and the flesh of ALL men, both free and bond, both small and great." Does not this look like a clean sweep; the destruction of all on earth? Who will be left? In this last great battle against Christ, we see on the one side Antichrist and his followers: the false prophet and church dignitaries; all on earth on one side, and all in heaven on the other side. "And the Beast was taken, and with him the false prophet that wrought miracles before him, with which he deceived them that had received the mark of the beast, and them that worshipped his image." So, according to the Word, both the Antichrist and his chief Bishop, were taken alive and cast bodily into a lake of fire burning with brimstone. This will positively, literally take place when Christ comes to reign. These are all facts, literal

THE MARRIAGE OF THE LAMB 215

facts: "Things that must come to pass." "And the remnant," men still remaining on earth after all the warring and judgment plagues have done their work, "were then slain with the sword of Him that sat upon the horse, which sword proceedeth out of His mouth."

He who made the heavens spoke the WORD, and all men fell dead before Him, women and children may be excepted. "And all the fowls were filled with their flesh." There were none left to bury the dead. All men are dead. This is exactly how things are going to close up in this old world, and close up soon.

It seems clear, from the prophecy of Zech. 14:16-19, that a remnant of each of these nations that fight in the Antichrist army, shall remain on earth; and shall go up to Jerusalem from year to year to worship the King, the Lord of hosts; and to keep the feast of tabernacles. Probably some men and many women and children who have not been forced to take the mark of the beast, and worship the image, because of their isolated homes, or some other reason, will remain, a remnant, to perpetuate their nations during the millenial reign of Christ on earth; but all will be in subjection to Christ and His Kingdom.

BINDING SATAN

AND I saw an angel come down from heaven, having the key of the bottomless pit and a great chain in his hand. And he laid hold on the dragon, that old serpent, which is the Devil, and Satan, and bound him a thousand years, and cast him into the bottomless pit, and shut him up, and set a seal upon him, that he should deceive the nations no more, till the thousand years should be fulfilled: and after that he must be loosed a little season. Rev. 20:1-3.

Christ has come to reign. He has destroyed his enemies. The Antichrist and false prophet, with all their followers, are gone. Satan, who had led them all to ruin, is still here. An angel came down from heaven having the key to the bottomless pit. There is a bottomless pit, and Satan is bound with a chain and cast into that pit, the door is closed, locked, and sealed. He remains there for one thousand years, while Christ reigns on this earth, where Satan had reigned for six thousand years. The Lamb has overcome him, and the saints have overcome him. He shall deceive the nations no more till the thousand years be fulfilled. There are to be nations again on this earth during the reign of Christ. At the time of the flood there were but eight persons left alive upon the earth, but in four hundred years, in Abraham's day, there were many nations on the earth, all descendants of Noah. When Israel rejected Christ and crucified Him, it was cut off and the Gospel was given to the Gentiles. But Israel is to be grafted in again; not all of it, but *believing* Israel. "And they also, if they abide not still in unbelief shall be grafted in: for God is able to graft them in again." Romans 11:23.

God always had a remnant in Israel who believed. "What saith the Scriptures? I have reserved to myself seven thousand men who have not bowed the knee to the image of Baal. Even so at this present time also there is a remnant, according to the Election of Grace." Romans 11:4-5. God said to Isaiah "Though the number of the children of Israel be as the sand of the sea, a remnant shall be saved. For God will finish the work, and cut it short in righteousness: because a short work will the Lord make upon the earth." Rom. 9:27-28. The Lord's remnant in the days of the Antichrist is 144,000 men and women, twelve thousand of each of the twelve tribes of Israel. God saved equal numbers of male and female to repopulate the earth in the days of Noah, and it is reasonable to suppose that He will have equal numbers of male and female to re-populate the earth during the Millenial Reign.

The 144,000 were sealed in their foreheads by an angel, at the very time the saints were resurrected and caught up into heaven. This remnant of Israelites were present on earth when the evil spirits were let loose out of the bottomless pit to torment men for five months; but they were immune. They were carried away into the wilderness into a place where they were fed of God during the whole reign of the Antichrist. They were immune to all that came upon the earth. They, as Noah was brought out of the Ark after the flood, will be brought out of their hiding place and grafted into the true olive tree, after the Antichrist has been destroyed and Satan is bound and cast into the bottomless pit.

These Israelites are twelve nations, and will be judged by the twelve Apostles sitting upon twelve thrones (see Matt. 19:28). "And Jesus said unto them, Verily I say unto you, that ye which have followed me, in the regeneration when the Son of Man shall sit in the throne of His glory, ye also shall sit upon twelve thrones judging the twelve tribes of Israel." There will always be at least twelve nations on earth during the thousand years of Christ's reign on earth, perhaps many more. There are Scriptures that indicate that Gentile nations may be in existence during the Millenium, but no man who takes the mark of the beast will be left alive in the earth. None of the nations will be deceived by the devil during the thousand years.

And I saw thrones, and they sat upon them, and judgment was given unto them; and I saw the souls of them that were beheaded for the witness of Jesus, and for the Word of God, and which had not worshipped the beast, neither his image, neither had received his mark upon their foreheads, or in their hands: and they lived and reigned with Christ a thousand years. But the rest of the dead lived not again until the thousand years were finished. This is the first resurrection. Blessed and holy is he that hath part in the first resurrection: on such the second death hath no power, but they shall be priests of God and of Christ, and shall reign with him a thousand years. Rev. 20:4-6.

After Satan was cast into the bottomless pit, John saw another scene, seemingly here on the earth. He saw thrones; the twelve thrones upon which the twelve Apostles sat. Judgment was given unto the Apostles to judge the twelve tribes of Israel. Then he saw the men, and probably women, too, who had been beheaded because they had witnessed for Jesus and believed and obeyed the Word of God, and had not worshipped the beast, neither his image, neither had received his mark upon their foreheads or in their hands. "And they lived and reigned with Christ a thousand years." Here we have positive evidence that the beheaded saints who died rather than sin against God and their own souls, were also resurrected and reigned with Christ: but the rest of the dead, that is the unsaved, unbelieving dead, lived not again; were not resurrected until the thousand years were finished. This is the closing scene of the first resurrection.

"Blessed and holy is he that hath part in the first resurrection: on such the second death hath no power, but they shall be priests of God and of Christ and shall reign with Him a thousand years." Observe, this blessing is to them who are holy, for "without holiness, no man shall see the Lord."

> And when the thousand years are expired, Satan shall be loosed out of his prison, and shall go out to deceive the nations which are in the four quarters of the earth, Gog and Magog, to gather them together to battle; the number of whom is as the sand of the sea. And they went up on the breadth of the earth, and compassed the camp of the saints about, and the beloved city: and fire came down from God out of heaven, and devoured them. And

BINDING SATAN

the devil that deceived them was cast into the lake of fire and brimstone, where the beast and the false prophet are, and shall be tormented day and night forever and ever. Rev. 20:7-10.

With one bound we pass from the beginning to the end of the reign of Christ on the earth, without another glimpse of the conditions then existing. We find some of those conditions in other Scriptures. At the end of the thousand years Satan is let out of his prison and appeared again on the earth. He goes forth to deceive the nations which are in the four quarters of the earth: Europe, Asia, Africa and America. "Gog and Magog." This term refers to persons who do not know God, hence can be deceived. When men know God they will not be deceived by the devil. The devil controls all whom he can deceive. Now he gathers them together to battle against Christ and the saints here on the earth.

This army which Satan has gathered is as numerous as the sand of the sea. Here is a strange scene. At the close of a thousand years of blessedness on earth, with no devil to tempt, with Christ and the saints to help, this great number do not know God: have not been born of God; are in their natural, fallen, human state, without God and without hope. They are in the condition of a son or daughter, born and reared in a godly home, where the Scriptures are read and prayer offered by the parents, but the children have not yielded themselves to God. So these godless children become the prey of the devil, and are led to fight their only Saviour and true friend. They went up from all quarters toward Jerusalem, where Christ will sit on David's throne. They compass the camp of the saints about, the beloved city, Jerusalem. Fire comes down from God out of heaven and devours them. All these poor deceived people become ashes under the feet of God's children. There shall be left unto them neither root nor branch. (Read Malachi 4:1-3).

The devil that deceived them was cast into the lake of fire and brimstone, where the beast and the false prophet were cast a thousand years before. Satan had been in the bottomless pit for a thousand years before this, but was not anihilated. Now his fate is not anihilation, but to be tormented day and night forever and ever. This lake of fire is the place where the Antichrist and the false prophet are. They, too, have spent a thousand years there and are not yet anihilated.

THE GREAT WHITE THRONE

AND I saw a great white throne, and him that sat on it, from whose face the earth and the heaven fled away; and there was found no place for them. And I saw the dead, small and great, stand before God; and the books were opened: and another book was opened, which is the book of life: and the dead were judged out of those things which were written in the books, according to their works, and the sea gave up the dead which were in it; and death and hell delivered up the dead which were in them: and they were judged every man according to their works. And death and hell were cast into the lake of fire. This is the second death. And whosoever was not found written in the book of life was cast into the lake of fire. Rev. 20:11-15.

Satan and his army are all disposed of: Satan, in the lake of fire, together with his army, their bodies in ashes, their souls in hell. The seven thousand years of man's existence on this earth has nearly ended. The people who are yet in the body on earth, mostly, if not all, Israelites, are saints; holy people that Satan could not move. The earth is now cleansed by removing all things that offend; for "The Son of Man shall send forth His angels and they shall gather out of His Kingdom all things that offend, and them which do iniquity: and shall cast them into a furnace of fire: there shall be wailing and gnashing of teeth." Matt. 13:41-42. This having been done; God's week having ended (the seven thousand years); the judgment is next in order. "Once to die, and after that the judgment."

The Last Resurrection

The sea gave up the dead which were in it, and death, that mysterious monster, death, delivered up the dead which were in death (this refers to the body), and hell delivered up the dead which were in it (this refers to the soul). And the living saints of that day will be changed in a moment into the resurrected state. And I saw the dead, soul and body, small and great, stand before God and His throne. "And I saw a great white throne, and Him that sat on it, from whose face the earth and the heaven fled away." The judgment will not be on this earth, as there would not be room for all the people who have lived on the earth to stand on this earth. *All will be there*. The judgment will probably be in the air. At this time "The heavens shall pass away with a great noise, and the elements shall

THE GREAT WHITE THRONE 225

melt with fervent heat, the earth also and the works that are therein shall be burned up." 2 Peter 3:10.

The earth having passed away, all the human beings that have ever lived upon the earth are gathered together and stand before the GREAT WHITE THRONE to be judged, to give an account of the "deeds done in the body," or while they lived on earth. "And the books were opened." First, God's word; second, the records of deeds done in the body; third, the book of life; and the dead were judged out of those things which were written in the books, according to their works. There will be no jury, there will be no lawyers, there will be no witnesses. God will judge according to the things written in the books, according to the life they lived in the body.

"Marvel not at this: for the hour is coming, in which all that are in the graves shall hear His voice; and shall come forth; they that have done good, unto the resurrection of life; and they that have done evil, unto the resurrection of damnation." John 5:28-29.

The people are separated, right and left: two great companies, and the sentences are all announced. In one company all God's children; all those who are born of God, have overcome the world, the flesh, and the devil: in the other company, all who were not born of God, but who had yielded themselves up to gratify their desires, with the world, the flesh, and the devil. Then death, that incomprehensible thing called death, was cast into the Lake of Fire, where the Antichrist, the False Prophet, and the Devil had been cast. Closely following this, *HELL,* that place and condition where the unrepentant sinner goes at death, and from which he came to be judged, hell is cast into the Lake of Fire.

This Lake of Fire is the *second death.* When the body went into the ground and the soul into hell, the person was in the *first death.* "And whosoever was not found written in the Book of Life was cast into the Lake of Fire." Then they were both soul and body in the *second death.* Being dead in trespasses and sins, and having persistently refused to be made "Alive to God, through Jesus Christ our Lord," they have remained spiritually dead, until the body dies, and is resurrected, and then both soul and body, they go into the Lake of Fire.

O my God! will this arouse the reader, so that he will repent and turn to God with all his heart, and be made alive to God, through Jesus Christ our Lord.

All this that John saw, this Revelation of things that must come to pass at the time appointed, will surely be enacted to the very letter. No deception here. God deals in facts, and in mercy and love reveals those facts to us that we may be saved. "Turn ye, turn ye, for why will ye die, O house of Israel." Ezek. 18:31.

When the Son of Man shall come in his glory, and all the holy angels with him, then shall he sit upon the throne of his glory: and before him shall be gathered all nations: and he shall separate them one from another, as a shepherd divideth his sheep from the goats: And he shall set the sheep on his right hand, but the goats on the left. Then shall the King say unto them on his right hand, Come, ye blessed of my Father, inherit the kingdom prepared for you from the foundation of the world: for I was a hungered, and ye gave me meat; I was thirsty, and ye gave me drink: I was a stranger, and ye took me in: naked, and ye clothed me: I was sick, and ye visited me: I was in prison, and ye came unto me. Then shall the righteous answer him, saying, Lord, when saw we thee a hungered, and fed thee? or thirsty, and gave thee drink? When saw we thee a stranger, and took thee in? or naked, and clothed thee? Or when saw we thee sick, or in prison, and came unto thee? And the King shall answer and say unto them, Verily, I say unto you, inasmuch as ye have done it unto one of the least of these my brethren, ye have done it unto me. Then shall he say also unto them on the left hand, Depart from me, ye cursed, into everlasting fire, prepared for the devil and his angels: for I was a hungered, and ye gave me no meat: I was thirsty, and ye gave me no drink: I was a stranger, and ye took me not in: naked, and ye clothed me not: sick, and in prison, and ye visited me not. Then shall they also answer him, saying, Lord, when saw we thee an hungered, or athirst, or a stranger, or naked, or sick, or in prison, and did not minister unto thee? Then shall he answer them, saying, Verily, I say unto you, inasmuch as ye did it not to one of the least of these, ye did it not to me. And these shall go away into everlasting punishment: but the righteous into life eternal. Matt. 25:31-46.

THE NEW EARTH

AND I saw a new heaven and a new earth: for the first heaven and the first earth were passed away; and there was no more sea. Rev. 21:1.

The scenes before us in this chapter are all beyond the "Great White Throne Judgment." All the dead on earth, or in the sea, and all that were in hell, have been raised from the dead; and have stood before the throne, and have been judged, and sentenced, and sent away; and all, whose names were not found written in the Book of Life were cast into the Lake of Fire.

Our study in this chapter is about the new home of God's children, after the judgment. The Lord Jesus told the disciples that in His Father's home there was abundance of room. That He was about to leave them and go to His Father's home, to prepare a place for them. "And if I go to prepare a place for you, I will come again, and receive you unto myself; that where I am, there ye may be also." John 14:3. We are now studying about this place our Lord has prepared for us.

The beloved disciple, and apostle, declares, "And I saw a new heaven and a new earth: for the first heaven and the first earth are passed away; and the sea is no more." This new earth is a second earth, in that he declares, "The first heaven, and the first earth, have passed away."

The Apostle Peter gives us quite a full description of the passing away of this earth. "But the heavens that now are, and the earth, by the same word, have been stored up for fire, being reserved against the day of judgment, and destruction of ungodly men. * * * But the day of the Lord will come as a thief; in which the heavens shall pass away with a great noise, and the elements shall be dissolved with fervent heat, and the earth and the works that are therein shall be burned up. Seeing that these things are thus all to be dissolved, what manner of persons ought ye to be, in all holy living and godliness, looking for and earnestly desiring the coming of the day of God, by reason of which the heavens being on fire shall be dissolved, and the elements shall melt with fervent heat." 2 Peter 3:7, and 10-12. R. V.

Here we have a new earth, with its heaven, and surroundings, prepared, and specially prepared as a home for the sons of God.

It is declared of the saved children of Abraham, "These all died in faith, not having received the promises, but having seen them afar off, and were persuaded of them, and embraced them, and confessed that they were strangers and pilgrims on the earth. For they that say

THE NEW EARTH

such things declare plainly that they seek a country. And truly, if they had been mindful of that country from whence they came out, they might have had opportunity to have returned. But now they desire a better country, that is, a heavenly: wherefore God is not ashamed to be called their God: for He hath prepared for them a city." Heb. 11:13-16.

Here we see clearly that the old patriarchs knew of this New Earth and City. They did not seek any country or city on this earth.

On this new earth there will be no sea, with its everlasting moanings, and dreadful storms, and separating into nations the inhabitants of this earth. The new earth will be so glorious in all its arrangements, in size and wondrous beauty, that God, our Father, will move His Capitol, and throne from its present location, on to this new earth; and God Himself will dwell with men who have been washed in the Blood of the Lamb.

This scene occurs after the judgment. The earth with all the works of man is gone, has passed away, is out of existence, and a new earth appears. "And I saw a new earth, and on it there was no sea." The first earth was two-thirds sea; but the new earth is to have no sea. In the fifth verse we read, "He that sat upon the throne said, Behold, I make all things new. And he said unto me, Write: for these words are true and faithful." This is not a renovating, or purifying, or a remodeling of this earth, for this earth is under sentence of fire. It was destroyed by water, and it will be destroyed by fire. The Lord Jesus declared, "Heaven and earth shall pass away, but my word shall not pass away," and God said to John, "I make all things new." "These words are true and faithful." There will not be one atom of matter in that new earth that ever was in any other planet. God's children in their glorified state will rank next to God. He is our Father, not theoretically, but really; and we are heirs by birth; legitimate sons. And God has made a new planet, greater, more beautiful, more wonderful than any other planet in the universe. He had none already made such as He determined to be the everlasting home of His Sons and Daughters, so He said, "I make all things new." So we can look forward to this beautiful new home.

> And I, John, saw the holy city, new Jerusalem, coming down from God out of heaven, prepared as a bride adorned for her husband. And I heard a great voice out of heaven saying, Behold, the tabernacle of God is with men, and he will dwell with them, and they shall be his people, and God himself shall be with them, and be their God. And God shall wipe away all tears from their eyes; and there shall be no

THE NEW EARTH

more death, neither sorrow, nor crying, neither shall there be any more pain: for the former things are passed away. And he that sat upon the throne said, Behold, I make all things new. And he said unto me, Write: for these words are true and faithful. And he said unto me, It is done. I am Alpha and Omega, the beginning and the end. I will give unto him that is athirst of the fountain of the water of life freely. He that overcometh shall inherit all things; and I will be his God, and he shall be my son. But the fearful, and unbelieving, and the abominable, and murderers, and whoremongers, and sorcerers, and idolaters, and all liars, shall have their part in the lake which burneth with fire and brimstone: which is the second death. Rev. 21:2-8.

The Holy City

"And I, John, saw the holy city, New Jerusalem, coming down from God out of heaven, prepared as a bride adorned for her husband." This is the city of God, the Capitol of the Universe. The throne of God is in it it, and the temple of God is there. The gold paved streets are there, and God is there. The Capitol City of the Universe is being moved bodily from its former location or orbit, to the New Earth. I, John, saw it coming down out of heaven to the *new earth,* is implied. Who for a moment would suppose that God would move the New Jerusalem onto this small earth, that has been almost a hell ever since men have lived on it. We believe that the present location of heaven is the best in all the Universe for situation, until this new earth has been made for God's children, with special view of moving the Capitol to it, as soon as the children of God are ready to occupy it. Listen to what God told Isaiah about it:

"For, behold, I create new heavens, and a new earth, and the former shall not be remembered nor come into mind." Isaiah 65:17.

This is a new creation, a better location for the City of God. The saints in that new home will not so much as remember that they ever were on this little marble of a planet, that man can compass in a few months; that has been covered with human blood. *"This earth shall be burned up."*

The *Holy City,* as it came down, was in all its virgin beauty, as in the day it was made.

"And I heard a great voice out of heaven saying, *Behold the tabernacle of God is with men, and He will dwell with them."* Before the judgment men had dwelt with God in heaven, but God had prepared something better, and now moves His Capitol, and Throne, to the better sphere. This new earth far outshines every other planet made. "And they shall be His people, and God himself shall be with them,

THE NEW EARTH

and be their God." God shall wipe away all tears from their eyes, and pain, and sorrow, and crying, and death, will be unknown, for the former things are passed away. "And He said unto me, It is done. I am Alpha and Omega, the beginning and the end. I will give unto him that is athirst of the fountain of the water of life freely. He that overcometh shall inherit all things; and I will be His God and he shall be my son." This is to be the portion of God's sons and daughters. O, to be a Son of God! What a wonderful thing it will be to become a Son of God!

This is the City that Abraham looked for, "For he looked for a City which hath foundations, whose builder and maker is God." Heb. 11:10. And it is written of the ancient saints, "God hath prepared for them a City." And Paul said, "Here we have no continuing City, but we seek one to come." Heb. 13:14. And again, "Ye are come unto the City of the living God, the heavenly Jerusalem." Heb. 12:22. "He that overcometh shall inherit all things." The new earth and the new heavens; and the New Jerusalem.

"But the fearful, and unbelieving, and abominable, and murderers, and whore-mongers and sorcerers, and idolaters, and all liars, shall have their part in the lake which burneth with fire and brimstone: which is the second death."

The first death is dreadful, *but O! the second death.*

> And there came unto me one of the seven angels which had the seven vials full of the seven last plagues, and talked with me, saying, Come hither, I will shew thee the bride, the Lamb's wife. And he carried me away in the spirit to a great and high mountain, and shewed me that great city, the holy Jerusalem, descending out of heaven from God, having the glory of God: and her light was like unto a stone most precious, even like a jasper stone, clear as crystal; and had a wall great and high, and had twelve gates, and at the gates twelve angels, and names written thereon, which are the names of the twelve tribes of the children of Israel: On the east three gates; on the north three gates; on the south three gates; and on the west three gates. And the wall of the city had twelve foundations, and in them the names of the twelve apostles of the Lamb. Rev. 21:9-14.

One of the seven angels that had the seven last plagues, and had poured them out, went to John, and asked him to go with him, and he would show him the *Bride, the Lamb's wife.* He carried John away in the spirit to a great and high mountain and showed him that great City, the Holy Jerusalem, descending out of

THE NEW EARTH

heaven from God. What a sight that must have been as it glided out into space with all its brilliancy and glory. *"Having the glory of God."* The city itself had the glory of God. Who can imagine? Who can conceive the greatness of that glory? The bride was in that city, being carried in all its gorgeousness to her new home, the New Earth.

And he that talked with me had a golden reed to measure the city, and the gates thereof, and the wall thereof. And the city lieth four-square, and the length is as large as the breadth: and he measured the city with the reed, twelve thousand furlongs. The length and the breadth and the height of it are equal. And he measured the wall thereof, an hundred and forty and four cubits, according to the measure of a man, that is, of the angel. And the building of the wall of it was of jasper; and the city was pure gold, like unto clear glass. And the foundations of the wall of the city were garnished with all manner of precious stones. The first foundation was jasper; the second sapphire; the third, a chalcedony; the fourth, an emerald; the fifth, sardonyx; the sixth, sardius; the seventh, chrysolyte; the eighth, beryl; the ninth, a topaz; the tenth, a chrysoprasus; the eleventh, a jacinth; the twelfth, an amethyst.

> And the twelve gates were twelve pearls; every several gate was of one pearl; and the street of the city was pure gold, as it were transparent glass. Rev. 21:15-21.

Here we have all the beautiful stones and crystals, and gold and pearls, used to give us some small idea of the beauty of the city. But human language and earthly things all fail to show forth its glory. How oft has its glory been told, but what must it be to be there?

> And I saw no temple therein: for the Lord God Almighty and the Lamb are the temple of it. And the city had no need of the sun, neither of the moon, to shine in it: for the glory of God did lighten it, and the Lamb is the light thereof. And the nations of them which are saved shall walk in the light of it: and the kings of the earth do bring their glory and honour into it. And the gates of it shall not be shut at all by day: for there shall be no night there. And they shall bring the glory and honour of the nations into it. And there shall in no wise enter into it anything that defileth, neither whatsoever worketh abomination, or maketh a lie: but they which are written in the Lamb's Book of Life. Rev. 21:22-27.

The Lord God Almighty and the Lamb are the temple of it, and they also are the light of it.

The saved from the different nations shall walk in the light of that city, and the Kings who are saved, bring their glory and honour into it; and the gates are never shut, for there is no night there. And they shall bring the glory and honour of the saved of all nations into it. Only glorious and honourable things will be there. And there shall in no wise enter into it anything that defileth, neither anything that worketh abomination or maketh a lie, but they which are written in the Lamb's Book of Life.

THE HOLY CITY

AND he shewed me a pure river of water of life, clear as crystal, proceeding out of the throne of God and of the Lamb. In the midst of the street of it, and on either side of the river, was there the tree of life, which bare twelve manner of fruits, and yielded her fruit every month: and the leaves of the tree were for the healing of the nations. And there shall be no more curse: but the throne of God and of the Lamb shall be in it; and his servants shall serve him: and they shall see his face; and his name shall be in their foreheads. And there shall be no night there; and they need no candle, neither light of the sun; for the Lord God giveth them light: and they shall reign forever and ever. Rev. 22:1-5.

These statements are not to be spiritualized as applying to Christian experiences or attainments in this life: they belong to the City of God, and to the New Heaven, and the New Earth in the *WORLD TO COME*. There will be a pure river of the *WATER OF LIFE*, clear as crystal, proceeding out of the throne of God,

THE HOLY CITY

and of the Lamb. This river flows down the center of a great street, of width appropriate for a such a city, having a population of billions of saints. On either side of this river, and on this street of tremendous width, were trees of life. A river of life, with trees of life, to emphasize Eternal Life. On the trees twelve varieties of fruit; and a new crop every month. No famine there, and no dried, or canned, or stale fruit; and no one will tire of the food. The leaves of the trees fill the whole atmosphere with the ozone of health, keeping the saints from all nations in perpetual health.

"And there shall be no more curse." Thorns and thistles and weeds, the earth refusing to yield her fruit; caterpillers and locusts, and all the curse that came on this earth because of sin, will be absent from that new home, that holy, happy world to come. The throne of God and of the Lamb shall be in that City, on that New Earth, and His servants shall serve Him with a real, sincere, heart, love service. They shall see His face, and His name shall be in their foreheads. God himself shall fill that city with the purest holy light, and there the saints shall reign forever and ever.

> And he said unto me, These sayings are faithful and true: and the Lord God of the holy prophets sent his angel to shew unto His servants these things which must shortly be done. Behold, I come quickly: blessed

is he that keepeth the sayings of the prophecy of this book. Rev. 22:6-7.

These sayings are absolutely true; God, Himself, will faithfully perform and bring to pass all things herein revealed. Blessed is the man who believes and consequently keeps the sayings of the prophecy in this book.

> And I, John, saw these things, and heard them. And when I had heard and seen, I fell down to worship before the feet of the angel which shewed me these things. Then saith he unto me, See thou do it not: for I am thy fellow-servant, and of thy brethren the prophets, and of them which keep the sayings of this book: worship God. And he saith unto me, Seal not the sayings of the prophecy of this book: for the time is at hand. He that is unjust, let him be unjust still: and he which is filthy, let him be filthy still: and he that is righteous, let him be righteous still; and he that is holy, let him be holy still. Rev. 22:8-11.

"I, John, saw these things and heard them." This was not a dream or phantom. "And when I had heard and seen, I fell down to worship;" to thank God for revealing all these wonderful truths concerning the things which must certainly, positively come to pass. And God commanded John, saying, *"Seal not the sayings of the prophecy of this book."* To seal them would be to write them in such ambiguous language that the reader could not understand them. But he was to write them down plainly, so that all might know the truth. For the time is at hand. "He that is unjust, let him be unjust still; and he which is filthy, let him be filthy still; and he that is righteous, let him be righteous still: and he that is holy, let him be holy still." Here is a solemn truth stated. There is a point of time in every man's life when he crosses the Rubicon, and his condition remains unchanged forever; as unjust, filthy, righteous or holy. This does not look like a second chance or after-death salvation. *Be warned and turn to God now.*

And, behold, I come quickly; and my reward is with me, to give every man according as his work shall be. I am Alpha and Omega, the beginning and the end, the first and the last. Blessed are they that do his commandments, that they may have right to the tree of life, and may enter in through the gates into the city. For without are dogs, and sorcerers, and whoremongers, and murderers, and idolaters, and whosoever loveth and maketh a life. Rev. 22:12-15.

"I come quickly; and my reward is with me." Have you observed that this book of Revelation commences and ends with this saying? Everything between, with the exception of the first five chapters, has direct reference to His coming and the things that will transpire after His coming. "My reward is with me." The righteous will begin to reap their reward from the time of His coming, on and on forever. He who is the Alpha and Omega, the beginning and the end, the first and last, the Almighty, has revealed all these things.

Obedience to God, doing His commandments, is absolutely necessary for admission to the Holy City. "They shall have right to the tree of life, and may enter in through the gates into the City." "Faith without works is dead." But the following classes of persons are excluded from this City,—the dogs, human dogs, sorcerers, whoremongers, idolaters, those who love to tell lies—all these will have their part in the *Lake that burneth with fire.*

I, Jesus, have sent mine angel to testify unto you these things in the churches. I am the root and the offspring of David, and the bright and morning star. And the Spirit and the bride say, Come. And let him that heareth say, Come. And let him that is athirst come. And whosoever will, let him take the water of life freely. Rev. 22:16-17.

Here Jesus Christ declares that he sent an angel to declare all these things to the Churches, that they might know what was to come to pass upon the earth. God, Himself, will not change this program of events that He has given unto

THE HOLY CITY

men. "These words are true and faithful." Rev. 21:5. "I am the Lord, I change not." Mal. 3:6. He declares that He is the root and the offspring of David, that is, the true Messiah, and the Bright and Morning Star.

The Holy Spirit says, Come, to every sinner: Come to Christ and receive Eternal Life. And the bride, the holy people, say, Come to Christ and be saved. And God says, Let him that heareth these invitations say to their fellows: Come away from sin to God. And let him that is thirsting for happiness come to Jesus. And whosoever will, all over the earth, let him take the water of life freely, without money and without price, a free gift.

> For I testify unto every man that heareth the words of the prophecy of this book, If any man shall add unto these things, God shall add unto him the plagues that are written in this book: and if any man shall take away from the words of the book of this prophecy, God shall take away his part out of the Book of Life, and out of the holy city, and from the things which are written in this book. He which testifieth these things saith, Surely I come quickly, Amen. Even so, come, Lord Jesus. The grace of our Lord Jesus Christ be with you all. Amen. Rev. 22:18-21.

And now God testifies to every man that heareth the words of the prophecy of this Book of Revelation, not to add to, or take from the words of the book of this prophecy, or God shall add to him the plagues herein mentioned, and take away his part out of the Book of Life, and out of the Holy City. All true saints the world over should continually say, "Come, Lord Jesus, come quickly." All who are ready "Love His appearing."

THE LITTLE HORN.

I CONSIDERED the horns, and behold, there came up among them another little horn, before whom there were three of the first horns plucked up by the roots: and behold, in this horn were eyes as the eyes of a man, and a mouth speaking great things. * * * I beheld then, because of the voice of the great words which the horn spake, I beheld even till the beast was slain, and his body destroyed, and given to the burning flame. * * * I saw in the night visions, and behold, one like the Son of man came with the clouds of heaven, and came to the Ancient of days, and they brought Him near before Him. And there was given Him dominion, and glory, and a kingdom, that all people, nations, and languages, should serve Him: His dominion is an everlasting dominion which shall not pass away, and His kingdom that shall not be destroyed. * * * And of the ten horns that were in his head, and of the other which came up, and before whom three fell; even of that horn that had eyes, and a mouth that spake very great things, whose look was more stout than his fellows. I beheld, and the same horn made war with the saints, and prevailed against them; * * and the ten horns out of this kingdom are ten kings that shall arise; and another shall rise after them; and he shall be diverse from the first, and he shall subdue three kings. And he shall speak great words against the Most High, and shall wear out the saints of the Most High, and think to change times and laws: and they shall be given into his hand until a time and times and the dividing of time. But the judgment shall sit, and they shall take away his dominion, to consume and to destroy it to the end. Dan. 7:8, 11, 13-14 and 20-21 and 24-26.

All these Scriptures refer to the Anti-Christ and his kingdom.

The ten horns mentioned in the twenty-fourth verse do not refer to the fourth beast or Roman Empire. Neither do they refer to a restored Roman Empire; but they indicate ten kingdoms that spring out of the fourth beast, or Roman Empire.

Daniel was very anxious to know about the ten horns that were in the fourth beast's head; "and of the other little horn that came up before whom three of the ten horns fell," or "Were plucked up by the roots." See verses nineteen and twenty. The little horn had eyes, and a mouth that spake very great things; and this horn was more stout than any of the ten horns.

THE LITTLE HORN 249

Daniel was enquiring into the meaning of the horns, more than of the Roman beast itself. And he is anxiously considering this little horn that made war with the saints; and prevailed against them; until the Ancient of days came, and the judgment was given to the saints of the Most High; and the time came that the saints possessed the kingdom. Verses twenty-one and twenty-two.

And Daniel "Went near one of them that stood by, and asked him the truth of all of this. So he told me, and made me know the interpretation of the things." Verse sixteen. Thus he said, "The fourth beast shall be the fourth kingdom upon the earth, which shall be diverse from all kingdoms, and shall devour the whole earth, and shall tread it down, and break it in pieces. And the ten horns out of this kingdom are ten kings that shall arise: and another shall arise after them; and he shall be diverse from the first, and he shall subdue three kings. And he shall speak great words against the Most High, and he shall wear out the saints of the Most High, and think to change times and laws: and they shall be given into his hand until a time and times and the dividing of time." Verses twenty-three, four and five.

These ten horns are the present kingdoms of Europe, and Asia, that came out of the Roman Empire. And those kingdoms are the ten toes of the great image that Nebuchadnezzer saw in his dream. See Dan. 2:31-45.

The little horn with eyes and a mouth, has not yet arisen among the ten kingdoms of Roman origin. But it will spring up among them, and shall subdue three kings, or pluck up three horns by the roots.

This little horn is the Anti-Christ. He is not one of the Kings, but another horn, or king, more stout than any of the ten kings. He comes up as a little horn, and finally becomes the greatest.

The Lord Jesus will not come, until this little horn makes its appearance. Begins to grow up. This is the man of sin. II Thes. 2:3-4.

We find some remarkable statements concerning this man of sin, in Dan. 11:36-45.

> And the king shall do according to his will; and he shall exalt himself, and magnify himself above every god, and shall speak marvelous things against the God of gods, and shall prosper till the indignation be accomplished: for that, that is determined, shall be done.
>
> Neither shall he regard the god of his fathers, nor the desire of women, nor regard any god: for he shall magnify himself above all.
>
> But in his estate shall he honour the God of forces: and a god whom his fathers knew not shall he honour with gold,

THE LITTLE HORN 251

and silver, and with precious stones, and pleasant things.

Thus shall he do in the most strongholds with a strange god, whom he shall acknowledge and increase with glory; and he shall cause them to rule over many, and shall divide the land for gain.

And at the time of the end shall the king of the south push at him: and the king of the north shall come against him like a whirlwind, with chariots, and with horsemen, and with many ships; and he shall enter into the countries, and shall overflow and pass over.

He shall enter also into the glorious land, and many countries shall be overthrown: but these shall escape out of his hand, even Edom, and Moab, and the chief of the children of Ammon.

He shall stretch forth his hand also upon the countries: and the land of Egypt shall not escape.

But he shall have power over the treasures of gold and silver, and over all the precious things of Egypt: and the Libyans and the Ethiopians shall be at his steps.

But tidings out of the east and out of the north shall trouble him: therefore he shall go forth with great fury to destroy, and utterly to make away many.

And he shall plant the tabernacles of his palace between the seas in the glorious holy mountain; yet he shall come to this end, and none shall help him.

This Anti-Christ is to make his appearance, and rule over a small people, having obtained rulership over a kingdom by flatteries. "And after the league made with him, he shall work deceitfully." Dan. 11:21-23.

ISRAEL TO BECOME A NATION.

THE Israelites are to again become a Nation, having been scattered among the nations for two thousand years.

This European War has brought about a willingness to let the Jews have their own land; and a National existence. Jerusalem has been wrested from the Turk; and the Jews are aroused as never before, since their dispersion. And they are planning and organizing to take possession of Palestine, as soon as assurances are given then from the present Rulers of Europe, that they may have autonomy. And this may come to pass at any of the Allies' War Councils, as a war measure. Calling all Jews from all parts of the earth, to come to Palestine; and arm themselves to hold their country.

The Jews have the men and the money to do this; and they will do it with a vim that will astonish the world. They will establish a Republic; and elect a President; and that President will be of the tribe of Judah, and perhaps of the House of David; and that President will be the Anti-Christ, coming in by flatteries; and making a covenant with the people for seven years, the full term, or tenure of office for President; and in the midst of the term of office he will have developed his true character as the man of sin, having actually sat in the newly erected Temple in Jerusalem, and declared himself to be the only God, or above all gods. He will then cause the daily sacrifices to cease; and will pollute the altar, probably by burning a sow upon it.

Then the Jews will break their covenant with him; and attempt to depose him. By this time the ten kingdoms, or horns, having by the assistance and guiding hand of the Anti-Christ, subdued and plucked up three horns, or kingdoms; and having completed a Confederation of ten horns with ten crowns, they will make the President of the Israelitish Republic, King over them all. Having been fully satisfied, seeing his great wisdom, and ability in organizing and governing the Israelites, together with his superhuman miraculous powers, that there is no other such man on earth.

The little horn will then "Speak great words against the Most High; and shall wear out the saints of the Most High; and think to change times and laws; and the saints shall be given into his hand until a time and times and the dividing of times. Dan. 7:25. This is just forty-two months, or twelve hundred and sixty days, or three years and a half, in which he will do his awful work of destroying all who will not take his mark, and worship the image he will set up. This is the Great Tribulation.

The last part of this chapter came to me in the night, during the first part of February, 1918; and it has pressed upon me with such persistency that I feel impelled to write it. I am not a prophet; and I know nothing of myself. The theory herein advanced seems reasonable; and quite probable. If it proves to be true, the people living at the time of its fulfillment will know that the Lord gave it to me. And they will have more confidence in this whole book.

The Jews rejected the Lord Jesus Christ, when He came unto them, in His father's name. And Jesus said unto them, "I am come in my Father's name, and ye receive me not: if another shall come in his own name, him ye will receive." John 5:43. The Anti-Christ will come in his own name, and the Jews will receive him as their Messiah.

THE STAR OF BETHLEHEM.

THIS book was typewritten in December, 1917; but no money was in sight to publish it, the Author having laid up no treasure on earth to draw from. Having preached the Gospel for fifty years; and having reached his seventy-seventh birthday, was fasting and praying before God for three days, without eating any food. And the Lord made it known to him that this book was to be, as the Star of Bethlehem was to the wise men from the East, so this book would be to thousands of men and women who will be left behind, when the Lord comes and resurrects the righteous dead; and translates the living saints. This books will help to bring them to Christ, their only hope.

The Lord also made it clear that we should, under the guidance of the Holy Spirit, write special instruction to the people left on earth who must go through the Great Tribulation, or die as martyrs in it.

We feel continual sorrow for the preachers, and people who once knew the Lord, and were happy in His love; but who have accepted the

THE STAR OF BETHLEHEM

Devil's offer made to Jesus Christ. "The Devil taketh Him up into an exceeding high mountain, and showeth Him all the kingdoms of the world, and the glory of them; and said unto Him, All these things will I give thee, if thou wilt fall down and worship me." Matt. 4:8, 9.

Christ had come to this earth to destroy the works of the Devil, and take possession of it, and reign over it. And save the people by means of His death on the cross. And the Devil showed Him an easier and quicker way, to obtain all earthly good and glory: hoping to blind His eyes to the future eternity of happiness, or misery.

This same temptation comes to every man and woman after they are born of God: as they meet the opposition from the world and the devil; and find that "All that will live godly in Christ Jesus, shall suffer persecution." II Tim. 3:12. Then Satan presents an easier way. He has thousands of ministers, and college professors, busy deceiving young converts, by showing them how to become all things to all men so as to escape the cross of crucifixion to the natural, carnal, fleshly desires for ease, and worldly honour, and wealth. And so, the world is filled, or has in it millions of people who were once God's children, and happy in Him, who have accepted the pleasures, and riches, and honours of a godless world; and have lost all the joys of salvation, and fellowship with the

Father and His Son Jesus Christ. I John 1:3.

These people have a form of godliness; but deny the power of God to save from all sin, and keep one pure in heart, unto the coming of the Lord Jesus Christ. I Thess. 5:23. Those millions of people are now in their autos, and beautiful homes, rolling in ease, and wealth, or seeking with all their might to do so, not knowing the "Signs of the times" that the Lord has already arisen to "Shake terribly the earth." Isa. 2:19. And to "Destroy them that destroy the earth." Rev. 11:18.

Jesus Christ said to the Jews, "O Jerusalem! Jerusalem! which killest the prophets, and stonest them that are sent unto thee; how often would I have gathered thy children together, as a hen doth gather her brood under her wings, and ye would not. Behold your house is left unto you desolate: and verily I say unto you, Ye shall not see me, until the time come when ye shall say, Blessed is He that cometh in the name of the Lord." Luke 13:34-35.

THE EARTH LYING IN RUINS.

DEAR READER: I heartily sympathize with you in your terrible distress: as the whole world lies in ruins on every side; but your precious life has been spared. No tongue can describe the awfulness of conditions about you. You only see what is next to you, but you see such conditions as never existed before.

It is not necessary to tell you that there has been an earthquake. You know what has taken place where you are. The whole world is in a similar condition. And all of this is because of sin.

The long-suffering and merciful God of heaven and earth, who has given men two thousand years of warning, and patient wooing, has now commenced to "destroy them that destroy the earth," that He may raise up a people who will serve Him in spirit and in truth.

You were at one time, a true child of God, and happy in His service; but you did not go on to perfection. You did not give all diligence to make your calling and election sure. You saw the faults of other people, but would not see, and cry out to God about your own faults.

You would not forsake all, and be separated unto the Lord. You loved the world more than you loved God. You loved the applause of the world; and failed to seek for the honour that comes from God only. You know what you lived for. And now Christ has returned to the earth, and has raised the righteous dead; and translated the righteous living. They are all gone to be forever with the Lord; and you are left.

I deeply sympathize with you; and am anxious to show you the only way of escape. It is back to Jesus, the only Saviour. The everloving Jesus. He longs for you. He died for you. He bought you with His blood. He tried to get your attention away from your business planning, and worldliness, and make you ready for His return. And even now He is trying to save you, before other coming Judgments fall on you. Repent! Repent! Repent! Let your eyes flow with tears, and your heart break with sorrow, for your rebellion against God. And now quickly fall on your face before Him; and cry out to God for mercy. He will hear you. He wants you to come. Return unto the Lord and He will return to you. He says, Return unto me and I will return unto you. O! the goodness and mercy of God!

There is nothing but sorrow before you on this earth; and but a little time to stay here. The devil and the Anti-Christ will soon be on

THE EARTH LYING IN RUINS

your track, and will kill you, unless you curse Jesus, and worship the image set up. Pray! Pray! Pray!

Let Us Reason Together.

You have probably read this book all through; if not, do so now. Let it be a guiding star to bring you back to Jesus, the only Saviour.

You know that the European war was followed by famine; and the famine was followed by pestilence; and that the wild beasts did their part in killing over a fourth part of the earth. All of this was according to the Scriptures referred to in this book. You know that the world earthquake has come, moving even mountains and islands out of their places; and that the sun became black as sackcloth of hair; and the moon became as blood; and the stars fell from heaven to the earth; and the world is lying in ruins. And you know that multitudes are dead and dying all around you. And if you will make careful enquiry, you will find that every deeply spiritual person is gone. That all the worldly-minded persons, like yourself, are still here, unless they were killed in the earthquake. But their bodies are with you. Now search, and you cannot find the body of a true saint on the earth. They are all resurrected, and caught up to be forever with the Lord. They are now in heaven with God. All of this has been foretold in this book; but you disregarded it. Now you see that it is all true.

Now that all the saints are gone, terrible judgments will fall upon the wicked, rebellious people that remain; and you will go down with them, unless you quickly repent, and obtain mercy; even then you will probably die as a martyr, at the hands of the wicked. There is no time for delay. Hurry! Hurry! Hurry!

The next thing before you is a world fire, in which one-third of the world will be burned up; and one-third of the trees, and all growing crops. This will bring a dreadful famine; and tremendous loss of life everywhere. And the next judgment will turn one-third part of the sea into blood; and every living thing in that part of the sea will die; and all ships and crews in that part of the sea will be destroyed. Now the third judgment comes quickly, turning one-third of all fresh water into wormwood, so that many who drink of the waters will die. If you are not convinced that I am telling you the truth: when these judgments fall on the earth, they will convince you. Study carefully what judgment is to come next; and when it comes, you will know that God is not dead, or slack concerning the fulfillment of the Scriptures. Every word will come to pass. All prophecy will be fulfilled.

Read this book through very carefully, and note what God has revealed. "The things that

THE EARTH LYING IN RUINS 263

must come to pass." And they will come to pass just as declared in the Scriptures.

From the enthronement of the Anti-Christ, to the destruction of the Anti-Christ, and his followers, will be forty-two months, or three and a half years. So you have but a short time to live on this earth. And remember, if you take the mark of the beast, so as to get bread, or for any other cause, you will doom yourself to eternal torments. Read carefully Rev. 14:9-11. "If any man worship the beast and his image, and receive his mark in his forehead or in his hand, the same shall drink of the wine of the wrath of God, which is poured out without mixture into the cup of his indignation; and he shall be tormented with fire and brimstone in the presence of the holy angels, and in the presence of the Lamb: and the smoke of their torment ascendeth up forever and ever: and they have no rest day nor night, who worship the beast and his image, and whosoever receiveth the mark of his name."

FINIS

Jesus is Coming Soon

Dear Friend:—Spread the news. Tell it far and wide. You have probably read this book through, if not, read it. You are, or ought to be deeply impressed concerning the days in which we live: and the awful things that are coming upon the earth. Should you not bestir yourself and spread the news? Your relatives and neighbors must not be left in darkness concerning the awful tribulation just before us. And the coming of the Lord Jesus Christ.

Are you willing to put five, ten, or twenty dollars into these books, and circulate them among your friends. And keep them going, until the whole town knows about those things that Christ died to bring to our ears?

The Antichrist will soon have all the property you own. Spend some of it now for the salvation of men while you can. How many books can you use? Write for wholesale rates.

We want hundreds of Agents in every State in the Union.

WILLIAM FRANCIS MANLEY,
1616 New Jersey St.

Los Angeles, California.

Trieste Publishing has a massive catalogue of classic book titles. Our aim is to provide readers with the highest quality reproductions of fiction and non-fiction literature that has stood the test of time. The many thousands of books in our collection have been sourced from libraries and private collections around the world.

The titles that Trieste Publishing has chosen to be part of the collection have been scanned to simulate the original. Our readers see the books the same way that their first readers did decades or a hundred or more years ago. Books from that period are often spoiled by imperfections that did not exist in the original. Imperfections could be in the form of blurred text, photographs, or missing pages. It is highly unlikely that this would occur with one of our books. Our extensive quality control ensures that the readers of Trieste Publishing's books will be delighted with their purchase. Our staff has thoroughly reviewed every page of all the books in the collection, repairing, or if necessary, rejecting titles that are not of the highest quality. This process ensures that the reader of one of Trieste Publishing's titles receives a volume that faithfully reproduces the original, and to the maximum degree possible, gives them the experience of owning the original work.

We pride ourselves on not only creating a pathway to an extensive reservoir of books of the finest quality, but also providing value to every one of our readers. Generally, Trieste books are purchased singly - on demand, however they may also be purchased in bulk. Readers interested in bulk purchases are invited to contact us directly to enquire about our tailored bulk rates. Email: customerservice@triestepublishing.com

You May Also Like

Reports of the Board of Directors and of the Superintendents of the State Hospitals for the Insane at Raleigh, Goldsboro and Morganton, North Carolina

State Hospital of North Carolina

ISBN: 9780649690602
Paperback: 114 pages
Dimensions: 6.14 x 0.24 x 9.21 inches
Language: eng

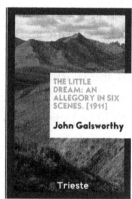

The Little Dream: An Allegory in Six Scenes. [1911]

John Galsworthy

ISBN: 9780649637270
Paperback: 50 pages
Dimensions: 6.14 x 0.10 x 9.21 inches
Language: eng

www.triestepublishing.com

You May Also Like

Hour by Hour; Or, The Christian's Daily Life

E. A. L.

ISBN: 9780649607242
Paperback: 172 pages
Dimensions: 6.14 x 0.37 x 9.21 inches
Language: eng

Report of the Second Annual Meeting of the Maryland State Bar Association, Held at Ocean City, Maryland, July 28-29, 1897

Conway W. Sams

ISBN: 9780649724185
Paperback: 130 pages
Dimensions: 6.14 x 0.28 x 9.21 inches
Language: eng

www.triestepublishing.com

You May Also Like

Report of the Department of Farms and Markets, pp. 5-71

Various

ISBN: 9780649333158
Paperback: 84 pages
Dimensions: 6.14 x 0.17 x 9.21 inches
Language: eng

Catalogue of the Episcopal Theological School in Cambridge Massachusetts, 1891-1892

Various

ISBN: 9780649324132
Paperback: 78 pages
Dimensions: 6.14 x 0.16 x 9.21 inches
Language: eng

www.triestepublishing.com

You May Also Like

Three Hundred Tested Recipes

Various

ISBN: 9780649352142
Paperback: 88 pages
Dimensions: 6.14 x 0.18 x 9.21 inches
Language: eng

A Basket of Fragments

Anonymous

ISBN: 9780649419418
Paperback: 108 pages
Dimensions: 6.14 x 0.22 x 9.21 inches
Language: eng

Find more of our titles on our website. We have a selection of thousands of titles that will interest you. Please visit

www.triestepublishing.com